FAMOUS ASSASSINATIONS

Sarah Herman

SAPERE
BOOKS

FAMOUS ASSASSINATIONS

Published by Sapere Books.

20 Windermere Drive, Leeds, England, LS17 7UZ,
United Kingdom

saperebooks.com

ISBN: 978-1-912786-67-1

Introduction

For the purpose of this book, it is necessary for us to understand what distinguishes an ordinary murder from an assassination, and what key ingredients a killing should entail for its inclusion in this collection. The assassination of President John F. Kennedy was one of the most famous public killings to occur in the twentieth century. As most readers will probably already be fairly familiar with the circumstances surrounding the Kennedy assassination, or at least have an image in their mind of the young president being shot while riding in an open-top car through the streets of Dallas, it is a simple example we can use to break down these key elements.

Oxford Dictionaries define 'assassinate' as 'to murder (an important person) for political or religious reasons'. Other historians have expanded the definition to include the requirement that the killing is a 'surprise' to the victim, ruling out preordained executions, however illegal or underhand they may be, and that it is a planned attack as far as the assailant is concerned. By examining this description of the term, we can determine whether Kennedy was truly 'assassinated' according to these guidelines.

— JFK was undoubtedly murdered when he rode into Dallas on 22 November 1963. The horrific shooting, witnessed by his wife, many Dallas locals who lined the road's grassy verges and millions of people around the world when the shocking footage of the attack was shown on television, was the murder of the decade and the first killing of a United States president for over sixty years.

— Without question, Kennedy was an important person whose name, political party, policies, decisions and personal life were known about all over the world. As the leader of one of the largest countries in the world at a time of great political and social change, what he stood for and the power he wielded was of huge importance to the American people. The notoriety and celebrity now fully associated with the President of the United States was less in Kennedy's day, but the growing popularity of television, live news coverage and the controversial decisions of the Kennedy administration, had made JFK one of the world's biggest political names.

— In order to qualify truly as an assassination, an individual's murder needs to have been motivated by reasons either political or religious. Debate on this point can be wide-reaching. With Kennedy, no one denies that his death was a planned act aimed at killing the president at a public event. His death was not an accident, or a random mistake made by a careless marksman. But the reason he was killed varies depending on whose side of the story you choose to believe. The man who was arrested for the attack and subsequently killed himself? The government? The witnesses who were silenced at the time and have since come forward? The conspiracy theorists and historians who have critiqued the short video film frame by frame to find evidence to support whatever theory they believe? The debate surrounding Kennedy's death is explored in more detail in Chapter Five, but it is certain there was some kind of political or ideological motive for Kennedy's death.

The most contentious part of the definition of assassination is the requirement for a 'political or religious motive'. The fact a politician is killed does not automatically mean the motive for their murder is political, and often the mental state of an assassin makes it questionable as to whether they had any real, rational motive at all, other than to kill a famous person for the attention and notoriety it would bring them. With dead assassins, guilty pleas and lack of evidence, it is often hard for lawyers, judges and the public to ascertain the true reason as to why the murder was committed. So, for the purpose of this book, some of these more obscure 'assassinations' have been included due to the high-profile status of their victims and the possible reasons for their deaths.

The term 'assassination' is derived from the name of a group of Nizari Ismaili Muslims, known then as the 'Hashishin', who operated between the eleventh and early thirteenth centuries in the Middle East during the Crusades. They were founded by Hassan-i Sabbah, an Ismaili preacher whose views went against those of other Shia Islam followers.

Hassan visited Persia (Iran) as a missionary, and soon found himself leading a cult of believers who chose to live in secrecy to protect their faith. Much of the Western world's perception and early knowledge of this group can be traced to Marco Polo's writings. He told of the legendary man who trained his supporters to be loyal to him. It was written that he would drug new recruits and take them into the exotic gardens of his training fortress, the Castle of Alamut, which was filled with beautiful women. The men believed they were in paradise and followed the words of their leader, on the promise that they would be able to return there. This secretive band of highly trained mercenaries, who were led by different men over the centuries, were extremely loyal to their group and were known for a number of assassination traits that are commonly associated with a contemporary view of an assassin. They usually approached their victims in public places, attacked quickly and then dissipated into the crowd. They wore disguises, indicated to their victims they were a target by leaving a dagger on their pillow, for example, and occasionally carried out suicide missions. Some murders were carried out for financial gain, but often religion and politics were the sole motives.

The monarchs, revolutionaries and secret agents who have followed the examples set by these Middle Eastern masters, and the Romans who preceded them, have killed to take over land and money, to gain power, to silence those who oppose or oppress them, for their religious beliefs and for the notoriety and attention to their political cause that comes with the murder of a high-profile victim. They have seen the extraordinary impact a terrifying assassination can have on a country and its leaders, whether the victim is loved or loathed by the masses. Of course, despite all these centuries of examples to learn from — too many to include in this book — almost all these deaths have one thing in common, and that is the futile nature of the assassination business.

After he learned of the death of American President Abraham Lincoln in 1865, British Prime Minister Benjamin Disraeli addressed parliament and stated, 'Assassination has never changed the history of the world', and if anything can be learnt from the tragedies chronicled here, it is that. The elimination of one man is not the elimination of a political party, a tyrannical dynasty, a revolutionary movement, or an idea that can live on long after one man's blood has been washed off the road.

Chapter One: When in Rome...

Liberty! Freedom! Tyranny is dead!
Run hence, proclaim, cry it about the streets
Julius Caesar (Act III, Scene I), William Shakespeare

When most people think of an assassination, they imagine the lone gunman striding brazenly forward to thrust a revolver into the belly of a leading politician, a rebel-rousing revolutionary or a royal or religious leader. The gunman is usually an unrecognisable face, unknown to the victim and the rest of the world until they commit the ultimate crime. They're rarely a politician themselves or a popular public figure, they don't control any armies or hold any titles, and they are certainly not related to the person whose life they choose to take.

This was not always the case. Ancient Greek and Roman civilisations may have laid the foundations for the modern world's cultural practices and political systems —governments, elections, democratic rule, etc. — but the realities of money, power and the men and women who traded in both were a far cry from the more civilised worlds they inspired. When all the power lies in the hands of a few, be it an ambitious monarch or a horde of influential senators, there will always be others waiting in the wings, ready to swoop in and take their place. For some, waiting for an ageing ruler to die peacefully in their sleep is more than their patience can handle, and a swift assassination is the most immediate way to take control. Of course, it is certainly not the most foolproof, as history, if not these men and women, has clearly shown us. Those who choose assassination along their route to the throne are often victims of an untimely death themselves.

While money and family connections can help contemporary politicians to progress in their careers, they are by no means the only factors that ensure political office and power. It would be ludicrous to learn, for example, that the British prime minister received his job title after ordering the death of the leader of the opposition. As other deaths in this book illustrate, state-sanctioned assassinations are still used by some modern governments and leaders to change political landscapes — especially in other countries than their own — but it is far less likely for a leader in the Western world to usurp their predecessor with a swift thrust of a dagger or a poisoned fruit plate. Powerful family dynasties in Ancient Greece and Rome were capable of wielding such influence, that anyone opposing them brought great risk upon themselves, meaning conspiracies and assassination plots were in some sense the safest way to bring about political change.

Philip II of Macedon (382 BC - 336 BC)

Victim

Despite his life ending with one of the most notorious assassinations of his day, Philip II of Macedon's name has never entered into the common consciousness as much as that of his son Alexander III, more commonly known as Alexander the Great. Philip was a warrior king of Macedonia, whose career had seen him work hard to keep alive his country's reputation as a strong military force. In 338 BC, two years before his untimely death, he led the Macedonian conquest of the Greek city states and declared that he would bring victory to his new allies in an invasion of Persian-ruled Asia. The Greeks regarded Macedonia as a barbaric northern nation, far beneath their civilised way of life, and Philip did little to refute the reputation: his bearded appearance was scruffy, he was scarred from his years of fighting and he had only one eye. The battles Philip saw in his military campaigns were mirrored by the troubles and rivalries of his home life — he may have been a king, but life at his castle was far from a fairy tale. Despite having seven wives by the age of forty-six, Philip still enjoyed the sexual attentions of many men, and there were many jealousies and disputes among his court.

Assassination

In spite of the Macedonians' barbarous reputations, Philip's daughter was married to the Greek king of Epirus in the summer of 336 BC, and the Macedonian king invited the rulers of the Greek states to come and celebrate the wedding. He was eager to show off the civilised celebrations by hosting banquets and athletic pursuits in honour of the marriage and the guests. The day after the wedding was dedicated to the games, which began with a procession of god-like statues being carried into the arena. An image of Philip was also included, an ambitious and presumptuous symbol of his perceived power and superiority. Philip was to follow the idols entering the stadium, without his usual bodyguards to prove his popularity, and present a solidified image of civilised Macedonia. As he approached the stadium, a bodyguard named Pausanias was standing in the entranceway. He lunged forward, as if to embrace the king, and then plunged a dagger into his ribs. Pausanias ran off to the getaway horse that was waiting, but never made it. He tripped on a vine and was dragged back to the arena and left to die by starvation.

Assassin

The Macedonian bodyguard who was waiting for Philip in the stadium entrance was allegedly one of the king's ex-lovers, who had been replaced in favour of another man, coincidentally with the same name. He had also suffered a humiliating and degrading rape by a relative of Eurydice, one of Philip's wives, and had received no justice, except for a promotion from the king for his pains.

Motives

Philip's assassination was planned, of that there was no doubt. Pausanias was ready and waiting, and he had planned to escape after the attack. The claims that Pausanias was one of Philip's lovers and that he alone was behind the assassination, came largely from an account written by Greek philosopher Aristotle, who acted as the private tutor to Philip's son, Alexander. If the stories of Pausanias's experiences are true, then there is good reason to believe Aristotle's account, but other historians have asserted that he acted under direct instructions from Philip's wife, Olympias. She had been Philip's favoured wife and Alexander was her son. At twenty-years-old, Alexander was proving himself a likely successor to his father, until Philip's seventh wife, Eurydice, gave birth to a baby boy. She had supplanted Alexander's mother as the king's favourite, and Olympias had tied the court, fearing for the future of her son. It's possible Olympias ordered the attack on her husband while Eurydice's son was still too young to take over from Philip, ensuring her own son's ascension to the throne. Some reports suggest she returned to the place where Pausanias was left to rot and placed a golden crown on his head, a remarkably unsubtle indication that she was in cahoots with, or at least supportive of, her husband's assassin.

Aftermath

There is no doubt Philip's assassination had a significant impact on the future of the ancient world. Had he lived to old age, and had Eurydice's son taken over from him, Alexander III may never have held a position of power or become the leader that he did. Taking the torch from his father, who had planned to conquer Persian-ruled Asia, Alexander led armies of Macedonians and Greeks in a ten-year campaign to expand the Macedonian Empire and defeat their enemies, conquering the ancient world as far east as northern India, and Egypt to the south. The cultural and political future of an entire region was altered for centuries owing to Alexander's leadership, and indirectly by Philip's assassination.

The Greeks and their Macedonian friends certainly knew how to conquer land and kill each other, but it was the Romans who gave us one of the most famous assassinations of all time, the death of Julius Caesar. The civilised aesthetic of Roman rulers and politics harboured a dark underbelly of begrudging senators, impatient heirs and power-hungry schemers planning how they could overthrow one ruler, replace them with another and still maintain the legitimate façade, to keep the Roman people at bay.

Long before Roman emperors started signing up for, and falling victim to, the assassination business, an ambitious Roman senator named Sulla took full advantage of this method of permanently eliminating one's rivals. Sulla lived between 138-78 BC and fought to victory in a violent civil war in 82 BC. After bringing his legions to Rome and overpowering his rivals, he ruled as a dictator, eliminating anyone who dared to oppose him by posting proscription lists officially condemning individuals to death or banishment from Rome, often with bounties on their heads. It was estimated by one ancient writer that as many as 9,000 powerful and wealthy Romans were murdered on his orders. Not only did Sulla's methods of retaining power leave the senate lacking in opposition voices, it also freed up the dead men's assets for his own financial gain. He even formed a personal bodyguard from 10,000 of their slaves. Rather shockingly, Sulla did not come to a nasty end himself. Sensibly, he retired from politics a year before his death, paving the way for a host of other ambitious men to step up to the dictatorial plate.

Like father, like son?

While Philip II's death was a violent act witnessed by many, the death of his son — the most ambitious, powerful and successful army commander of his time — was relatively peaceful. Residing in Babylon at the time of his death in what is present-day Iraq, Alexander the Great was strategising future campaigns to invade and conquer Arabia. These plans would never be realised because, in the year 323 BC, at the age of thirty-three, Alexander fell ill after a banquet, developed a fever over several days and died. There are differing reports about the exact details surrounding Alexander's last days, and some suggestions of foul play. Worn out from years of fighting and travelling so far from home, Alexander's own army had mutinied against him and some were furious with their leader's adoption of so many foreign Persian customs. It would therefore be a fair assertion to make that the king's own generals poisoned him, but this claim has proved inconclusive. It is more widely believed that this 'great' man was brought down by a common illness such as malaria or typhoid, or some other localised fever.

Pompey the Great (106 BC - 48 BC)

Victim

The assassination of Pompey the Great (Gnaeus Pompeius Magnus) is less well chronicled than that of his political peer and later rival, Julius Caesar, but just because Shakespeare didn't write a play about his death, it doesn't make it any less worthy of mention. Following the tyrannical rule of the notorious Roman dictator Sulla, three of Rome's most powerful men consolidated their popularity and power against that of the Senate: Julius Caesar, Pompey and Marcus Crassus. Pompey was a Roman General and influential politician who had served with Sulla during the civil war and helped to crush the Spartan slave revolt, among other great victories. Following Crassus's death in battle in Syria in 53 BC, the allegiance fell apart, and Caesar and Pompey began competing for power. The senate was more fearful of Caesar's growing hold over the people, and supported Pompey in the conflict between the two generals, which eventually moved right into Italy, dividing Roman families as citizens were forced to choose sides. Five years later, the fighting moved through Italy and culminated in the Battle of Pharsalus in Greece where, despite Pompey's superior army — with almost 50,000 infantry to Caesar's 22,000 — Caesar was able to strategically outwit his opponent and lead his men to victory. Pompey fled, disgraced by the defeat.

Assassination

Twenty thousand of Pompey's men surrendered to Caesar and were spared death, as was Marcus Brutus, a nobleman who had sided with Pompey but was later invited into Caesar's inner circle. Pompey, now a fugitive, fled across the Mediterranean to Egypt, believing it was his safest option, as there were troops still loyal to him there. After arriving offshore at the capital, Alexandria, Pompey sent word of his arrival to Egypt's King Ptolemy XIII, seeking protection from the young pharaoh. Fearful of the repercussions of supporting one of Caesar's enemies, but unsure of Pompey's reactions if they refused protection, Ptolemy's advisers decided the best option was to kill Pompey. When the general was safely aboard the small vessel intended to carry him ashore, the signal was given for his execution, and he was stabbed to death.

Assassins

Pompey's fate was sealed as soon as he set foot on that boat. The signal for his execution was given by Pothinus, the pharaoh's eunuch political adviser, but the fatal blows were delivered by an Egyptian called Achillas and two Roman soldiers, one called Lucius Septimius, who had previously served Pompey in battle. Writing over 200 years later, Roman historian Cassius Dio describes how Ptolemy himself was too young to consider Pompey's request for protection, but that the decision of Pothinus, Achillas and Septimius to murder Pompey brought a curse upon them, with indication that they were killed not long after Caesar learned of their deed.

Motives

The advisers to Ptolemy, the most influential being Pothinus, were probably doing what they believed to be the safest thing for the political future of Egypt. There is good indication that Pompey headed to Alexandria to gather a new army, to try once again to defeat Caesar. Welcoming Pompey into the palace would have put Egypt in a vulnerable position. Ptolemy was already fighting a war against his own sister, Cleopatra VII, so avoiding Caesar's wrath by killing Pompey was probably a wise decision under the circumstances. Even so, Pothinus and Achillas would later plot to assassinate Caesar after he sided with Cleopatra and reinstated her as a joint ruler of Egypt.

Aftermath

According to Cassius Dio, Julius Caesar eventually arrived in Egypt — he had been pursuing Pompey — to learn the news of the assassination. He was brought Pompey's head and ring, and at the sight of them wept bitterly, exclaiming grief for his fellow countryman. He did not laud praise on the murderers, but rather commanded that Pompey's head be given a proper Roman burial. While Pompey's assassination was not carried out by Caesar, his death paved the way for Caesar to dominate Roman politics for many years, with no eligible opponents willing to try their luck against his vast army. Caesar would face Pompey's image for a final time at the scene of his own death when he fell, murdered, at the foot of a statue of Pompey.

Julius Caesar (approx. 100 BC - 44 BC)

No assassination in history has captured the minds of artists and writers, or haunted the dreams of dictators and tyrannical leaders, as much as Julius Caesar's. While the reason behind the removal of an all-powerful, unaccountable leader by those trying to bring about regime change is not difficult to fathom, the direct and brutal way Caesar faced his end, at the hands of his contemporaries and friends, has been the cause of much debate and study ever since. Through accounts written by ancient historians such as Plutarch, Suetonius, Cassius Dio and Appian, it is possible to piece together the events leading up to his dramatic death.

Victim

An ambitious and hardworking general and war-time strategist, Julius Caesar had proved himself as an able politician, with good public speaking skills, and he quickly climbed the political rungs to the position of Consul in 60 BC, forming an unofficial triumvirate with Pompey and Crassus. Upon Crassus's death and Pompey's assassination, he returned to Rome and was made a dictator for a period of ten years in 46 BC (this was later extended to 'perpetual dictator' or dictator for life when he returned from campaigns in Spain in 44 BC). This position, where one member of the senate rules alone to provide stability and decisive leadership, was usually reserved for times of national crisis, but Caesar managed to win over many of the people by bringing a level of peace and wealth to the city that had been absent, and, while some were secretly concerned by his growing power, honours continued to be bestowed upon this king-like figure — his month of birth was renamed 'Julius' (July).

While Caesar had publicly refused the title of *Rex* or 'King', he was being treated as such. Statues of him were erected in every Roman temple, a gold throne was built for him in the senate and he started wearing purple robes and a crown of golden laurel leaves, symbolic of the early Etruscan kings.

Assassination

Caesar's power had increased exponentially, and fear was spreading through the Senate as they saw the republic system beginning to crumble. Senators began gathering at secret meetings in one another's houses and the idea of an assassination emerged. It was decided a senate meeting would be the ideal place to carry out the attack, considering they were all senators and their presence at an official meeting in such large numbers would not be cause for concern. The timing of the assassination was crucial as Caesar had planned to leave Rome for a military campaign against the Parthian Empire on 18 March 44 BC, in the hope of fulfilling his desire to be declared king. If he returned victorious, it would be harder to convince the rest of the senate of the necessity of their actions, as none would dare oppose a 'king'. The date was therefore set for 15 March, known to Romans as the Ides, at a meeting of the senate in an anteroom at the Theatre of Pompey. It was not held at the old senate house, because this building had been burned down eight years earlier, so senate business was being held at this new location.

Assassins

To speak openly about a planned assassination of Julius Caesar to the wrong person was a dangerous business, but as small factions of angry senators heard they weren't the only ones with murder on their mind, they soon came together to plan the assassination. It is reported that there were more than sixty conspirators involved in the plot. There were three men who could be considered the ringleaders in the planning.

Gaius Cassius: Cassius and Marcus Brutus had sided with Pompey during the civil war, but their lives had been spared by Caesar. Despite this, Cassius continued to feel slighted by Caesar, whose power was growing. He was influential in recruiting his brother-in-law Marcus Brutus and many other wealthy senators to support the assassination plot. Historians have argued that, while Marcus Brutus opposed Caesar's ruling of Rome, Cassius opposed Caesar himself and planned the assassination to enact revenge on the leader he had personal animosity towards. He had always hated tyrants and once, as a boy, had fought with Sulla's son, Faustus, because Faustus had bragged about his tyrannical father's immense power.

Marcus Brutus: One of Brutus's ancestors had been involved in the exile of the last king of Rome, Lucius Tarquinius Superbus, nearly 500 years earlier. Brutus is portrayed by historians as a principled man who wanted to protect the republic from the tyrannical rule of Caesar. His mother was one of Caesar's most favoured mistresses, which has led some to believe that Marcus could have been Caesar's illegitimate son. It is clear that Caesar favoured Brutus. He had spared his life, invited him back to court, and that year gave him one of the most coveted positions. He had also been pre-selected over

Cassius for a consulship in three years' time. In contrast to Cassius, Brutus put aside his personal feelings towards Caesar to ensure the dictator was removed from power. The involvement of such a respected and popular figure in the senate legitimised the murderous plan and many senators agreed to be involved, largely on the basis that Brutus was running the show.

Decimus Brutus: As one of Caesar's most-trusted officers — Plutarch wrote that he was so trusted by Caesar that he was entered in his will as his second heir — Decimus played a key role in ensuring the assassination could take place. It was after Decimus's urging that Caesar decided to attend the senate meeting where his life would end. He was sent to Caesar's home when the ruler failed to appear, and convinced him that the senate would be offended if he did not attend. It is also written that Decimus told Caesar the senate was ready to vote in favour of Caesar being declared king of the provinces outside of Italy, and that if he didn't attend the meeting, it would leave the floor open for his enemies to make speeches against him.

Motives

The legacy left by the ancient kings of Rome made the people fear the very notion of a king or leader who presented themselves as such. Years of dictatorial rule had encouraged the people to value a more balanced system with their republican government. Although the majority of Rome's wealth and its power in the form of armies was held by a small minority of noble families who received their seats in the senate accordingly, the temporary nature of offices and titles, and the dual consulship, meant no one person was at the top for too long, and no one person could control the senate alone.

Aftermath

Rushing from the senate meeting room covered in Caesar's blood, and their own — many of the conspirators had been injured in the frenzied attack on their dictator — the senators poured onto the streets, creating a public uproar. The sight of these bloodied, dagger-brandishing noblemen caused people to run, hide and lock their doors in fear as the news of Caesar's assassination made its way about the city. But the reports over what the conspirators did next, vary. While some historians claim that the men fled in fear of their lives being taken in revenge, Plutarch describes Marcus Brutus leading the crowd to the Capitol and delivering a speech in which he justifies the assassination. He told the confused Roman people that, while the senators had sworn their allegiance to their dictator, their first allegiance was to Rome itself, and that if the tyrannical Caesar was not performing his duties as a dictator, they were not duty-bound to perform theirs. The crowd, appeased by this reasoning and won over by Brutus, apparently accepted the assassination of their leader.

The conspirators' post-assassination plan had been to throw Caesar's body into the River Tiber and confiscate his property, but perhaps because of their fear of returning to the scene under the watchful eyes of Caesar's loyal deputies, Mark Anthony and Lepidus, his body remained in the meeting room until it was removed to his house by his slaves. In their determination and detailed plotting of Caesar's death, the senators had failed to recognise the importance of Caesar's allies. Had they assassinated Mark Anthony and Lepidus as well, there would have been less public opposition to their deed. It was Mark Anthony who insisted on a full public funeral and public reading of Caesar's will. Some public favour was restored when it was announced that Caesar had bequeathed three pieces of gold to each citizen, and Mark Anthony delivered a powerful speech condemning the conspirators' actions. But it was the sight of Caesar's mutilated body being paraded through the streets that really ignited the crowd. They built a bonfire, setting the body alight and then, with flaming torches, headed to the homes of the conspirators to kill them. Marcus Brutus and Cassius were forced to flee, leaving Mark Anthony and Lepidus in charge of Rome, thus starting an epic power struggle between those who claimed they should be the next Caesar. Any hopes of reinstating a functioning republic were crushed.

Caesar had left most of his estate to his great-nephew Augustus (later known as Octavian), who was formally adopted as his son. Mark Anthony, Lepidus and Octavian battled it out to assert themselves as the next dictator, and then later reconciled to form the Second Triumvirate. They finally avenged Caesar's death by defeating the armies of Marcus Brutus and Cassius, and sentencing both men to state executions. Octavian, known as Augustus, would go on to be the first Roman emperor, ruling for forty-one years without one attempt being made on his life. But anyone who thought Caesar's assassination would be Rome's last, was sorely mistaken.

Beware the Ides of March!

There were a few people in Rome who had the right to declare 'I told you so' after they learned of Caesar's assassination. Despite Caesar's vast informant network (some of whom were involved in the plot), he failed to learn of the plans to kill him before it was too late. Here are just some of the bad omens and warnings that Caesar received before he arrived at the meeting hall.

— Prior to the meeting, Caesar sacrificed an animal to read its entrails — this was traditionally done as a form of prophecy. When Caesar cut open his animal, a heart couldn't be found. Believing this creature to be unnatural and a bad omen, Caesar was fearful of what it meant.

— Caesar's wife, Calpurnia, had a nightmare the evening before the meeting in which she cradled her dead husband in her arms. Distressed and shocked by her vision, she warned Caesar not to attend the meeting that day. Others report that her nightmare was not so literal and that she dreamed of a gable ornament on Caesar's home — a mark of adornment and distinction voted for by the senate — being torn down.

— Caesar was advised by doctors not to attend the meeting, probably because he had been feeling ill and his doctors were worried by a seizure, which most likely was an epileptic fit, known by historians as the falling sickness.

— The most well-known warning Caesar was given about what was to happen was from a soothsayer dressed in traditional purple robes. Plutarch wrote that, a few days before the meeting, the soothsayer had said to Caesar: 'Beware the Ides of March,' the day that the conspirators had planned to carry out his assassination. Upon making his way to the meeting, Caesar spotted the soothsayer in the crowd and proudly declared, 'Well, the Ides of March are come,' to which the soothsayer replied, 'They are come, but they are not gone.'

— At a dinner party held on the eve of his death, Caesar was being entertained by his trusted deputy and supporter Marcus Lepidus. When the discussion turned to what kind of death was the best, Caesar declared, 'Let it come swiftly and unexpectedly,' which it did, the next day.

— When Caesar was being led from his house towards the senate meeting, a slave tried to get to him, but the crowds were too big, so he made his way into Caesar's house and asked Calpurnia to keep him safe until Caesar returned, because he had important matters to report to him.

— Short of someone telling Caesar to his face that he was about to be assassinated, receiving the news in a scroll before heading into the meeting could have prevented Caesar's violent end. Some historians point to Greek philosophy teacher Artemidorus of Cnidus as the man who, being part of Brutus's inner circle and therefore knowing of the assassination plot, stepped forward and handed the scroll directly to Caesar, urging him to read it immediately and emphasising its importance. Apparently, Caesar, who usually passed these scrolls directly to his attendants, held on to the warning as he entered the hall, but never read it.

Caesar's final moments: blow by blow

Upon arriving at the meeting, the senators gathered round, paying their respects to Caesar. Tillius Cimber had presented a request to have his exiled brother returned to Rome. Other senators in favour of the petition stepped forward, surrounding Caesar as he made his way to a seat at the foot of a statue of Pompey. But Caesar turned down the request and tried to silence the growing anger of the crowd.

Tillius pulled Caesar's toga from his neck and threw it to the ground, a sign to his cohorts that the attack should begin.

The first wound was inflicted by Casca, who stabbed Caesar in the neck with a dagger. This was far from a fatal wound; perhaps Casca was overtaken by nervousness and the enormity of what was about to happen. Some historians say Caesar was able to grab Casca's dagger, and others say he took his own stylus and thrust it into Casca's arm.

A war hero himself, Caesar had been in countless fights and reacted quickly, lunging away from the crowd, but he was soon surrounded by the many senators who had agreed to support the assassination. They revealed their daggers and attacked him from all sides.

At some point, Caesar was stabbed in the stomach, Gaius Cassius stabbed him in the face and Marcus Brutus stabbed him in the groin. He received a total of twenty-three stab wounds.

Before Marcus Brutus's assault, it is believed that Caesar uttered his last words in Greek, '*kai su teknon*', meaning, 'You too, my child'. Afterwards, he slumped in front of the Pompey statue and died.

An assassin in the family

Even before Caesar's great-nephew Augustus (Octavian) became emperor, there were rumours he may have been involved in an assassination. While commanding several legions in Mutina (Modena) in northern Italy, Octavian had been backed by the senate to fight against Mark Anthony. He was accompanied by the Roman Consuls of 43 BC, Hirtius and Pansa. Rather surprisingly, both Romans died during the conflict. Hirtius in battle, and Pansa from wounds received during fighting. Claims were made that Octavian was behind both deaths. One writer recorded that Octavian struck Hirtius in the confusion of battle, while Pansa's physician was arrested and charged with poisoning him. While it's unlikely that the young Augustus engineered these two high-profile deaths, he did demand, and later took, the consulship their sudden ends left behind.

Despite his long and powerful reign and three wives, Octavian didn't have a son and he faced his final years without an heir in place. He was desperate for a blood relative to take over from him to ensure all the work he had done to reform the Senate, politics and armies of Rome would be continued. But, being the favoured heir to the empire was not a safe role to take, and the suspicious deaths of many of Augustus's possible successors show the truly dangerous nature of the Julio-Claudian dynasty.

Marcellus: Augustus may not have had any sons of his own, but he did have a daughter, Julia. If Julia was to produce a son, then he would have a bloodline heir to the empire. He married Julia to his sister's son, Marcellus, who was still in his teens. Unfortunately, before an heir was produced, Marcellus was struck down by illness and died.

Agrippa: Julia, left a widow, was quickly remarried to Caesar's close friend General Agrippa, who was twenty-five years older than her. Despite their age difference, and Agrippa's previous marriages, the couple had five children, including three boys, Gaius, Lucius and Agrippa Posthumus. When Gaius was just eight-years-old, General Agrippa, who was to stand in as heir-apparent until the sons came of age, died at the age of fifty-one.

Gaius and Lucius: Finally, Augustus's family had produced three worthy heirs, and, as the oldest two boys grew, they began to carve out their political and military futures. Neither of the boys, however, would become Emperor of Rome: Lucius was struck down by illness in the south of France, and Gaius, who had become Consul by the age of twenty-one, was wounded during a siege in Armenia. He died shortly after, within two years of his brother's death.

Octavian: While Octavian's death in AD 14 is not widely accepted as an assassination, some historians point the finger at his third wife Livia. Livia's two sons from a previous marriage, Tiberius and Drusus, were not considered worthy successors by Augustus. After the deaths of Gaius and Lucius, Augustus reluctantly adopted Tiberius in the hope that Tiberius's adopted son Germanicus (who was also Augustus's great-nephew) would be his ultimate successor. It appeared to Livia that Tiberius would succeed her husband until Augustus visited his grandson Agrippa Posthumus, perhaps in a last-ditch attempt to prepare him for the throne. Some historians believe Livia poisoned figs that her husband ate after he had picked them for himself from the orchard.

Agrippa Posthumus: Upon Augustus's passing, Tiberius was the new emperor, but he did not announce his stepfather's death until he was certain there would be no immediate challenge to the throne. Written orders were sent to the guards of Agrippa Posthumus, ordering them to kill him, which they did. Whether those orders were sent by Tiberius himself (who denied his knowledge of them to the Senate) or his mother Livia, is debatable.

Germanicus: Tiberius's adopted son, who was also the great-nephew of Augustus, outshone his father and seemed a likely successor to the throne. He was in Syria when he fell ill and died, and the Syrian governor Gnaeus Piso, who was immediately suspected of poisoning him, was arrested and tried for his murder. Gnaeus took his own life — a noble Roman death — but some believe he acted directly on orders from Tiberius, who felt threatened by the young, successful Germanicus.

Drusus the Younger: After Germanicus's death, Tiberius's next natural heir would be his only son, Drusus the Younger. He held one of the consulships but also succumbed to a sudden illness, dying in AD 23. Later, it emerged that his own wife had conspired with others to poison him, including the head of the Praetorian Guard, the very force dedicated to protecting the life of the emperor.

Caligula (AD 12 - AD 41)

Victim

It's never a good idea to declare yourself emperor when the current ruler is still alive, but that's precisely what Caligula did, as Tiberius lay dying. Caligula was the son of Augustus's great-nephew Germanicus and the nephew of Tiberius, and a favoured successor to the throne. So when Tiberius was declared dead in the seaside town of Misenum, after suffering from a long bout of illness, Caligula, who was with him, stepped outside to greet the crowd who hailed him as the next Roman emperor. Suddenly, a rumour spread that Tiberius had come around from fainting and was asking for food. He was not dead at all. The head of the Praetorian Guard quickly put an end to any confusion by smothering Tiberius with a pillow.

Caligula's real name was Gaius Caesar Germanicus, but his nickname 'Caligula' meaning 'Little Boot' was much more fitting once he came into power. He may have been only one man, but this 'boot' of Rome proceeded to kick and stomp on the city that had rewarded him with riches and power. While many rejoiced in his ascension to the throne, and believed Caligula would bring peace and stability after the tyrannical final years of Tiberius's rule, after suffering some kind of illness, Caligula developed tastes and beliefs far from the heroic and noble values senators had in mind for their new leader. While ancient historians may have exaggerated some of Caligula's behaviour, a consensual picture of him engaging in unusual sexual practices such as incest, referring to himself as a god and treating his favourite horse, Incitatus, as a king, are widely believed to be true. Caligula squandered his inherited wealth and the wealth of the Roman empire on lavish events and parties — he once paid for a fleet of ships to be covered in soil and wood to form a floating bridge around two miles long, just so he could parade across the water on his horse, dressed as Alexander the Great.

Assassination

While the circumstances surrounding Alexander the Great's death are uncertain, there is no denying assassins' involvement in the violent end experienced by Caligula. On 24 January AD 41, the day of his assassination, Caligula was attending an event at a theatre in Rome. The assassins planned to wait in a corridor that led out of the auditorium, and corner the emperor when he retired from the festivities for lunch. The men crowded into the corridor with their knives and swords but believed their plot may have been foiled when Caligula failed to appear. Eventually the emperor, who had stomach pains and was debating whether to have lunch, made an appearance. He stopped to talk to some performers from the show and that is when two of the plot's ringleaders, Praetorian officers Cornelius Sabinus and Cassius Chaerea, approached the emperor. Seconds later, the emperor was on his knees with a sword wound that severed his jaw bone. Immediately, the two guards were surrounded by the other conspirators who delivered their blows en masse. When Caligula shouted out that he was still alive, they attacked more ferociously, battering him until he lay dead on the ground. Unfortunately for Caligula, and as the assassins expected, the German bodyguards arrived too late to save the emperor, but when they saw what had happened, they attacked the assassins, killing some of them along with a few innocent bystanders. The Praetorian Guard was in chaos and Caligula's wife and daughter were quickly located in the imperial palace and murdered — his daughter's skull was crushed by her being swung against a wall.

By Jupiter!

Before Cassius Chaerea dealt the first blow that helped bring Caligula's life to a very abrupt end, Sabinus asked the emperor for the day's password. As they held the rank of Tribune in the Praetorian Guard, it was their responsibility to find out the daily password or watchword issued by Caligula. Often the emperor would use obscene and humiliating words to embarrass Chaerea, but on the day of his death, the password was 'Jupiter'. After he spoke this word, Chaerea replied, 'So be it!' raising his sword and striking Caligula on the head, splitting his jaw bone. Chaerea was referring to Roman god Jupiter's power to kill a man from the heavens.

Assassins

The two men who stepped forward to deliver the initial deathly blows to Caligula, were two of the men whose job it was to protect the Emperor of Rome. As members of the elite bodyguard force, the Praetorian Guard, Cassius Chaerea and Cornelius Sabinus had direct access to Caligula and knew of his whereabouts. Chaerea was described by Cassius Dio as 'an old-fashioned sort of man' and held personal feelings of resentment towards Caligula for calling him 'wench', even though he was 'the hardiest of men'. Caligula was forewarned by a soothsayer to beware of 'Cassius'. He wrongly believed he had to watch out for the Governor of Asia whose name was Gaius Cassius, a relative of the Cassius who assassinated Caesar. While Chaerea dealt the first blow, Sabinus was quick to follow, delivering a swipe with his sword that pushed the emperor to his knees. Cassius Dio also wrote that there was a large number of men privy to the plot to have Caligula assassinated; and many in favour. Among them was Gaius Julius Callistus, a freedman who had once been a close adviser of the emperor. Callistus may have turned on Caligula after he was named, perhaps incorrectly, as a conspirator in a previous assassination attempt, and had to beg for his life despite his close relationship with the ruler.

Motives

An eye for an eye, a tooth for a tooth, is a saying that could be applied many times over for the reasons behind Caligula's brutal murder. While some tyrannical and outrageous behaviour was almost to be expected from an Emperor of Rome, Caligula ruled with a sadistic, torturous and oftentimes insane hand, which had both common Romans and noblemen living in fear. Caligula was known for having people imprisoned, mutilated or even killed for the smallest of offences, or simply because he was in a bad mood. He routinely humiliated members of the Praetorian Guard and senators, and over his near four-year reign, made many personal enemies. There was another more practical reason his assassins wished him dead: he had loosened the Roman purse strings to a point where the riches of the world's wealthiest empire were being frittered away on lavish parties, buildings, baths, games, chariots and all manner of luxuries. One of the emperor's most expensive habits was drinking vinegar in which pearls had been dissolved. The people of Rome watched in disgust and terror as this bizarre emperor raised their taxes, threw away their wealth and treated them abominably. Something needed to be done.

Aftermath

Cassius Dio made a pithy remark that, after three years, nine months and twenty-eight days in power, Caligula finally learned by experience that he was not a god. That's not to say his power vanished with his pulse: despite his overwhelming unpopularity, most people were too scared to celebrate the news of his death, fearing it was an elaborate hoax set up by Caligula himself to weed out his enemies. Although many debates followed the assassination as to whether a democracy or monarchy should follow, there was a general consensus that Caligula's death was good for Rome. There was some bloodshed at the scene of the assassination by Germanic bodyguards loyal to Caligula, but the assassins were not executed — the next emperor, Caligula's uncle Claudius, even had them pardoned.

Die, Claudius

Caligula's successor, the fifty-year-old Claudius, may have been mocked by the court for his sickly appearance, shaky hands, and stammering voice, but he was by no means stupid. After witnessing the horrifying death of his nephew, he took precautions to ensure he wouldn't face the same end. Unfortunately, having everyone who approached him searched for weapons was not enough to prevent one of his wives assassinating him in AD 54.

It is believed by many that his fourth wife, Agrippina, wanted to make sure her favoured son, Nero, was Claudius's successor, so she had the emperor poisoned … twice. History disputes the precise details of Claudius's death, but it is thought by some that, the first time, she had his chief taster sprinkle poison on some mushrooms he ate, but when he only fell ill, she saw to it that the doctor finished him off with a deadlier version.

Animal testing

The art of the subtle assassination in Ancient Rome often involved the administering of deadly poisons, and, for this reason, was not always reliable. Mixed incorrectly, a poisonous substance could result in only a bad case of diarrhoea, and the victim's knowledge that someone wanted them dead. When Emperor Nero wanted to eliminate the competition — Claudius's son, Britannicus — he wanted to make sure the job was done properly. He sought the services of the same poison expert who had helped his mother bring about Claudius's end, and had her brew a lethal concoction. He tested it on a goat, which took five hours to die, so he had the expert boil the formula down to increase its strength. He then tested it on a pig and they watched as it dropped dead, followed not long after by Britannicus.

Like mother, like son

Assassinating your own mother can be tricky, especially if she is a bit of an expert in the murder business herself. When Nero's mother, Agrippina, who had killed her husband Claudius to ensure her son's future on the throne, became more of a hindrance than a help by openly disagreeing with him and siding with his enemies, he decided it was best she was out of the picture for good. But killing her wasn't easy. Here are some of the methods he tried:

— Agrippina knew a lot about poisons, and their cures, which was lucky, as Nero tried to poison her three times. Each time she took an antidote that enabled her to survive.

— Nero took things up a notch by rigging a device in her bedroom that would make the ceiling panels fall on her in her sleep. The plan was never completed, however, after Agrippina was tipped off about the plot.

— The most extravagant of Nero's assassination plans involved the construction of a sailing boat that would collapse under a rigged, weighted canopy. Nero invited his mother to a festival and saw to it her own boat was unseaworthy after an 'accidental' collision. He offered her the rigged boat for her return journey. When the mechanism was activated, Agrippina's servant was killed, but she managed to swim all the way to shore with a shoulder wound, while the vessel sank.

— The ambitious mother finally saw her end when Nero resorted to more reliable methods and sent a group of soldiers to her villa to kill her with their swords. Apparently, when they went to lunge for her with their swords, she cried out that they should strike her in her womb.

The assassination of one's peers for political change or control did not end with Nero, the last emperor of the Julio-Claudian dynasty. Ancient Rome's history is riddled with family members, senators, soldiers and servants who were willing to risk their own lives for the possibility of political change through murderous means. In the third century especially, when, over a period of twenty-three years, thirty different generals were declared emperor of Rome, the stability of government and leadership was elusive, in large part due to political killings and shifting allegiances. These killings dominated politics for years and, in some ways, were considered a legitimate way for men to rise to the top and maintain their power. And while monarchs and ministers in later European and North American courts and governments may not have embraced the tool of assassination to the same degree as the Romans, power shifts, power struggles and political differences have been, and still are, decided by swords, triggers and even poison, when those who believe change is necessary see no other way to bring it about.

Chapter Two: For God and King

Nearly all men can stand adversity, but if you want to test a man's
character, give him power
Abraham Lincoln

Romans justified the killing of tyrannical leaders because of their abuse of power and blatant disregard for the people. Of course, when a dynastic system is in place which gladly passes crowns, land and titles from one generation to the next, and when monarchs and rulers believe they were ordained by God for the position, it's very hard for their enemies to legitimately remove them from power by killing them, especially in such an open and obvious manner as the assassination of Julius Caesar, and still retain the support of the people. The situation becomes more complicated when those in power have been put there by the results of a national vote or a general consensus of favour.

Of course, if the dangerous tyrannical rule of Caesar didn't stop some sixty men agreeing to his brutal and confrontational end, then there's little reason to think that birth right and public opinion would stop the daggers, guns and bombs of the people who followed them in history. While most royal rulers, during the Middle Ages in Western Europe, escaped the threat of assassination, the sacrilegious slaying in 1170 of Thomas Becket, the Archbishop of Canterbury, remains one of the most defining events of the period: an ambitious king, frustrated by his loosening grip on the church, inadvertently orders his knights to kill the powerful priest who blocks his path to total control.

Eastern rulers faced the more obvious and growing threat of both the original assassins, splinter religious groups of Shia Islam, who carried out strategic political assassinations to ensure their survival, and the Japanese ninja.

The splintering of the Christian religion in the 1500s during the Protestant Reformation, saw religious allegiance increase as a motive for assassination. And an individual's beliefs, their abuse of power through religion or their support of one particular faith group over another, has been one of the underlying causes of many high-profile ideological killings ever since. The connection between church and state — power over politics, and power over the people through their religious beliefs — has made monarchs, politicians and preachers vulnerable to the assassin's weapon throughout history.

Thomas Becket (1118-70)

The story surrounding Thomas Becket's rise to the top of religious rankings, and his dramatic downfall at the hands of his killers, is full of the ingredients that make a gripping period drama. While the plot to kill Julius Caesar illustrates the risks involved when one man attempts to take away the power of many, Becket's death came about when one man tried to take power away from another, the sovereign king of England. But this wasn't simply a power struggle over money, land and politics, this was the power to control the church and its many followers.

Victim

Thomas Becket (later known as Thomas à Becket) was born to French parents who moved to England before Becket's birth in 1118. His father was a wealthy merchant and once held the important position of Sheriff of London. Becket's education took place in London and in Paris, and he worked as a clerk and accountant before being taken into the household of the Archbishop of Canterbury, Theobald of Bee, to be a clerk. Theobald saw great promise in Becket, who would accompany him to Rome in 1148. Later, he would be ordained as a deacon and archdeacon of Canterbury, and in 1155, when King Henry II was looking for a suitable candidate to fill the vacant position of Chancellor of England, Theobald recommended Becket, who was also close friends with the king.

As Chancellor, Becket held one of the highest official positions under that of the king, and his close connection with Henry meant he received gifts from those noblemen looking to win the king's favour. All official documents passed through his hands, and as a drinking buddy, sports companion and trusted friend and adviser of the king, Becket was in a position to wield much power over the way England was run. When Theobald died, Henry saw the opportunity to gain back some control over the church — Theobald had not always seen eye to eye with Henry — and so elected his close friend Thomas as the new Archbishop of Canterbury. Forty-four-year-old Thomas was reluctant to accept the position, fearing his good relationship with Henry would be pushed aside by matters of church and state. But on Henry's insistence, he was ordained a priest on 2 June 1161, and consecrated as Archbishop of Canterbury the next day.

Almost immediately, a change was noted in Becket's lifestyle and demeanour. He took his religious office extremely seriously and, despite being accustomed to a rich, lavish lifestyle, he engaged in a humble monastic life, swapped his expensive clothes for a monk's habit, lived off a simple and meagre diet and spent his nights in prayer. He was not interested in fulfilling the wishes of the king, but felt obliged to uphold the powers of the church. Henry and Becket went from being colleagues and friends to opposing forces, both hungry for power, both refusing to back down. They disagreed over issues relating to church revenue, jurisdiction, criminal church clerks and royal marriage (see 'Motives' for more) and eventually, Becket fled England for France. The quarrel led to Henry exiling 400 of Becket's family and friends, and to Becket using his power to excommunicate bishops and leading lay figures in England who supported Henry. Becket also tried to enforce an interdict, whereby English people would not be allowed to attend church, get married or have their prayers heard by a priest, while Henry, in retaliation, had his son crowned as the future king by the Archbishop of York, a ceremony only allowed to be performed by the Archbishop of Canterbury. Although attempts were made to resolve their disputes, neither party was willing to bend for the other. It was to be Becket's dramatic change in personality and blatant refusal to do as the king wished that would bring his life to its infamous conclusion.

Assassination

There are five historical accounts of the events that followed, but only one by an eyewitness known as Edward Grim (sometimes Gryme), a visiting cleric who was with Becket at the time of his death. Records differ slightly, but most are in agreement with the order in which events unfolded. On 28 December 1170, four of Henry II's knights met at Saltwood Castle in Kent, where, with their host, Baron Ranulf de Broc, they forged a plan of attack. The following day, the knights, accompanied by the Baron and some others, arrived at the archbishop's palace in Canterbury, adjacent to the cathedral. Ranulf de Broc guarded the gatehouse while the knights demanded to see Becket, and ordered him to revoke the excommunications he had ordered. He refused and an angry discussion ensued. The knights left the archbishop's chambers to retrieve their swords. They returned and broke their way into Becket's residence at dusk. Finding him no longer there — some of the monks had forced Becket to leave his home and move into the cathedral through the cloisters, although Becket did not allow any doors to be barred behind him — the knights drew their swords and turned towards the cathedral, believing they would find him within.

Barging their way into Canterbury Cathedral where vespers were being sung, they once again demanded to know the whereabouts of Thomas Becket, 'Traitor to the king and the realm'. Becket made no move to escape and showed himself to the knights, saying, 'Here I am, no traitor to the king, but a priest of God … What do you want with me?', to which one of the knights is believed to have replied, 'That you should die'. While Becket would have known his life was in danger, given his ongoing disagreements with the king, these words meant the subsequent murder of Becket was less of a surprise attack to him than many of the other assassinations in this book: Becket knew that his number was up, and the knights were not leaving until he was dead.

The knights then proceeded to attack Becket, and tried to drag him from the cathedral. While they were all prepared to murder Becket, they were uncomfortable doing the deed in the house of God. Some townspeople had begun to gather for evening worship, and Becket clung to a pillar, making it impossible for the knights to remove him as their actions became more public.

One of the knights brought his sword down on Becket's head. Grim tried to intervene to protect the archbishop, and his arm took some of the force, but Becket was still hit. The knights' swords came for him twice more, forcing him to the floor, where he lay bleeding. A final blow sliced through Becket's head with such force that the knight's sword snapped when it hit the stone floor beneath. In some retellings, a final sign of disrespect is shown to Becket when one of Ranulf's clerics stepped forward and kicked Becket's head so his brains scattered onto the floor. Becket was dead, his assassins were known knights of Henry II, and their murderous actions had been witnessed by God, and perhaps, more worryingly, by a number of Becket's supporters.

Assassins

The four knights who road to Canterbury to ensure that Becket wouldn't cause the king any more problems were Hugh de Morville, William de Tracy, Reginald FitzUrse and Richard le Breton. They had been stationed in Normandy with Henry when news reached the king of Becket's return to England and his excommunication of those men who had resided over Henry's son's coronation. Henry's anger and seeming desire to see Becket removed for good resonated with the knights, who believed it was their duty to kill the rebellious archbishop. They crossed the English Channel separately, so as not to arouse suspicion, and reconvened at Saltwood Castle in Kent, where they discussed their plan and set off for Canterbury. After the assassination, the four men fled to Yorkshire where they hoped to avoid punishment for their actions. Considering they murdered a soon-to-be saint, they got off pretty lightly. Their sentence came in the form of a pilgrimage to Jerusalem as penance for their sins. None of the knights survived the long, arduous journey.

Motives

Whether the four knights who brandished their swords at Becket had any personal animosity towards him is unclear, but it is widely accepted that they understood the king wanted Becket removed from his position as Archbishop of Canterbury, and that the most effective way to see he was no longer challenging Henry was to end his life. Becket had not been the archbishop Henry had hoped for. He had defied the king's wishes on matters both trivial and important, making it impossible for Henry to have real control over the church. He refused to consent to the Constitutions of Clarendon, a set of laws that attempted to take judicial power from the church and instil rules and legal practice more in line with what the king's grandfather, Henry I, had tried to achieve. Becket had also meddled in personal matters relating to the king. When Henry wanted his brother to marry a widowed countess, Becket refused permission on grounds of consanguinity. The animosity between the two led Becket to even threaten to excommunicate the king himself. When word reached Henry in France that Becket had evaded arrest on his landing in England and been warmly received back in Canterbury, and then learned of the letters his other clergy, including the favoured Archbishop of York, had received informing them of their new sentences of excommunication on Becket's orders, he flew into a rage and said something to the effect of 'Who will rid me of this troublesome priest?', referring to the people of his court as traitors for allowing a mere clergyman to treat him in this manner. He would later claim his words to be a hypothetical question and not a direct order.

Aftermath

Almost immediately after his death, Becket became a martyr. Monks, clerics and townspeople gathered round after the knights had fled and bound his head and placed his body on the altar. People took pieces of his bloodstained clothing and guarded them as holy relics, while monks tried to collect brain matter from the chapel where he was slain. Becket was eventually buried in the crypt of Canterbury Cathedral. His tomb became a place of pilgrimage and was said to be the site of a number of miracles. Three years after his assassination, Becket was canonised as St Thomas.

The aftermath of Becket's assassination didn't work out quite as Henry had planned, if indeed he had planned it. The king denied all knowledge of the plot to have Becket killed, and claimed his words were rhetorical and should not have been taken as a literal order.

The public didn't see it that way, and Henry was widely condemned for his treatment of such an important religious figure. The Pope ordered that Henry perform an act of public penance for his crime, casting a shadow of guilt on the monarch. The king was forced to walk through Canterbury barefoot, wearing nothing but a simple pilgrim's gown. When he arrived at the location of Becket's assassination, he kissed the stone floor and entered Becket's tomb where his confession was heard and he asked for forgiveness. His back was then lashed three times by every monk in the cathedral. The king may have been rid of the thorn in his side, but the battle between church and state would continue for many years to come.

In God's house

Becket's death shocked and appalled the nation, and Christians around the world as they learned of his assassination. The disdain for Becket's killers was compounded by the fact they ended his life in the cathedral. But Becket is not the only person to find himself face to face with assassins in a place of worship.

— **St Peter of Arbues:** This fifteenth century Spaniard and canon member in Saragossa worked as an inquisitor for the Spanish Inquisition in 1484. His role involved seeking out Jewish people who had converted to Catholicism but were secretly continuing their practice of Judaism; they were known as Marranos. The men hated him for the punishments he was inflicting on them and their families, and they plotted to kill him. In September 1485, while praying at the altar in Saragossa Cathedral, he was attacked by a group of hired assassins who inflicted several fatal wounds. He died two days later.

— **Alberta Williams King:** The mother of Rev. Dr Martin Luther King Jr., seventy-year-old Alberta was shot dead in Ebenezer Baptist Church, Atlanta by Marcus Wayne Chenault Jr., who came to Atlanta on a mission to kill black church ministers, whom he believed were a menace to black people. He hated Christianity and said he was following his God's wishes when he attended the morning service on 30 June 1974. He had intended to kill Alberta's husband, Rev. Martin Luther King Sr., who was presiding over morning worship. After the congregation had been welcomed, Chenault rose from the front pew and opened fire with two pistols. Mrs King was fatally struck while playing the organ, as was church deacon Edward Boykin.

— **George Tiller:** Anti-abortion activist Scott Roeder attended the Reformation Lutheran Church in Wichita, Kansas, on the morning of 31 May 2009, with the aim of assassinating American physician George Tiller. Tiller had regularly attended this church for years, and was standing in the entranceway handing out church bulletins and acting as an usher. The service had just begun when Roeder walked up to Tiller and shot him in the eye with a handgun. As Roeder fled the scene, he pointed the gun at two other men who tried to stop him. Tiller was one of only three doctors in the USA where a woman could be given an abortion in her third trimester, which he performed at his women's health clinic. The clinic had previously been bombed by protestors and Tiller had survived a shooting in 1993. Fifty-one-year-old Roeder was found guilty of first-degree murder, which carried a mandatory life sentence.

— Daniil Sysoyev: On 19 November 2009, Russian Orthodox priest Daniil Sysoyev was shot in the head and chest by a masked gunman outside St Thomas' Church in southern Moscow. Not long before his death, the thirty-five-year-old preacher had reportedly told Russian journalists that he had received fourteen death threats, which he believed were because of his work with Muslim migrants living in Moscow. He had baptised eighty Muslims and his work was considered radical among other Christian clergy, who traditionally avoided trying to convert other faiths, and *vice versa*. In March 2010, the lead suspect in the murder was delivered to a police station to determine his involvement in the assassination. He had connections with an Islamic spiritual leader. At the station, he put up an armed resistance, throwing a grenade into the building and opening fire on the officers. He was shot dead. Criminal experts provided evidence that the gun used in the police shooting was the same as the gun used to kill Sysoyev.

In bad faith

Religious leaders and the men who support their causes are not immune to the assassination game. If anything, those who preach words in the name of God that go against the status quo, or who promote the views held by dangerous and subversive groups, can find themselves inciting more public anger and hatred than politicians. Running a country can make you unpopular, but there's nothing quite like the power of a religious voice and those who oppose it to make you more so. With many religiously-motivated assassinations, the argument of right and wrong is null and void where God's will is concerned, and while not all of these victims were killed solely because of their beliefs, their positions, faiths and viewpoints played a huge part in their assassins' motives.

Pope Alexander VI (1431-1503)

The head of one of the most powerful and infamous families of its day was Rodrigo de Borja, a Spaniard who changed his family name to Borgia when he moved to Italy, to appear more Italian. He became Pope Alexander VI in 1492 after cunningly manoeuvring his way through the corridors of power at the Vatican. At this time, the papacy was less of a religious office than a hugely powerful and influential force in Europe, and this appointment made the Spaniard's family the most powerful in Rome. His son Cesare Borgia embraced this power and was believed to be responsible for a number of assassinations and attempts on the lives of personal and political enemies of his father and, according to some accounts, Cesare may also have been behind his father's death. While it is believed Alexander most likely died from the malarial plague that swept through Rome in the summer of 1503, some authorities think he was accidentally killed when he drank some poisoned wine his son had intended for the family enemy Cardinal Adrian Corneto.

Joseph Smith (1805-44)

Smith was the founder and original leader of the Church of Jesus Christ of Latter-day Saints. At the time of his assassination, he was also the Mayor of Nauvoo, Illinois, and had announced a bid for the presidency of the United States. He was being held in Carthage County Jail on the charge of treason against the state of Illinois: he had ordered the city marshal of Nauvoo to destroy the printing press of a newspaper that had printed stories about him practising polygamy and having too much power as the head of the Mormon church in a largely Mormon town, while also being the mayor. On 27 June 1844, while awaiting trial with his brother and some others in the jail, a mob with faces blackened by gunpowder, entered the building and burst into the room, firing at the prisoners. Smith's brother was shot in the face and so was he, but he jumped (or, in some reports, fell) from the window in a bid to escape. Accounts differ as to how Smith died: some reports say his still-live body was propped up against a wall, so the mob could use him for target practice. Five defendants were tried for the murders, but all five were found not guilty by an exclusively non-Mormon jury.

Count Folke Bernadotte (1895-1948)

Swedish diplomat Bernadotte was appointed by the United Nations to work as a mediator between the Jewish and Arab sides in the newly-created state of Israel. He had successfully arranged a 30-day ceasefire between them in June 1948, but his future plans for settling the dispute were unpopular on both sides, and members of a Jewish terrorist group called Lehi believed he was pro-Arab and had to be eliminated if their future hopes for Israel were to be achieved. On 17 September of that year, Bernadotte was travelling through West Jerusalem on his way to a meeting, when a Jeep blocked the road and prevented his convoy from continuing. Inside the parked car were four assassins wearing Israeli army uniforms — it would have appeared to the convoy that they had set up a random army checkpoint. Three of the assassins quickly got out of the Jeep and started firing at Bernadotte's car. He was hit six times and killed. Some members of Lehi were arrested in the aftermath of the attack, but they were eventually released. Swedish authorities condemned the Israeli investigation into the assassination as negligent and doubted whether they had really tried to bring Bernadotte's killers to justice.

Mahatma Gandhi (1869-1948)

The assassination of Mohandas Gandhi (Mahatma was an adopted name meaning 'great soul') when he was a frail seventy-eight-year-old man, ended the life of one whom many considered to be the 'father of India': Gandhi had protested peacefully for more than thirty years for India's independence from Britain, which had finally been achieved on 15 August 1947. Even in his old age, Gandhi continued to be involved in the politics of his beloved country: he had fasted in September 1947 and January 1948 to convince Hindus to stop their violent attacks on Muslims living in Calcutta and Delhi, with peaceful results. But not all Hindus welcomed Gandhi's peaceful approach, which failed to avenge the violent Muslim attacks on their communities. It was to be in a setting that epitomised Gandhi's peaceful approach to conflict resolution, a daily evening ritual where he prayed with pilgrims, where an assassin took his life. On 30 January 1948, Nathuram Godse, the editor of an extremist Hindu newspaper, approached Gandhi as he walked up the stairs to the platform at the end of his garden, from where he would conduct the prayer meeting. Godse fired three shots at him and Gandhi fell to the ground after being hit in the abdomen and twice in the chest, and he died almost immediately in the arms of his great-niece who had been walking with him. Five hundred people were in attendance and a lynching would have ensued if the police had not been so quick to take Godse into custody. Godse and a co-conspirator were condemned to death for the assassination, and five others received life sentences for their involvement. After Gandhi's death, the country was in shock, and nearly a million people lined the procession route on the day of his funeral. The number of massacres between Muslims and Hindus dramatically decreased — even in death, Gandhi had brought a period of peace to the nation.

Archbishop Oscar Romero (1917-80)

The outspoken Salvadoran Archbishop had received a number of death threats before he was assassinated, but turned down police protection. Fourteen days before his killers finally succeeded on 24 March 1980, a briefcase containing explosives was found near the pulpit from which he was planning to preach. None of these things deterred Romero, who believed strongly that the El Salvador military were out of control and violating the human rights of the people they were being paid to protect. The country was facing civil war as left-wing rebel groups who wanted reform struck out against big business and the military; so the army, backed by US money, hit back hard, trying to crush the uprising and anybody whom they deemed to be a reformist. The archbishop preached about these wrongdoings in church and on the radio, but nothing changed. His killer, who remains unknown, arrived in a chauffeured, red Volkswagen car outside the Divine Providence Cancer Hospital in San Salvador, where Romero was conducting mass. He rested the rifle on the open car door and, aiming through the chapel door and down the centre aisle, he shot the archbishop once in the heart, climbed back into the car and drove away. Romero fell to the ground, blood covering his face as the nuns of Divine Providence rushed to his aid, but it was too late — he had been silenced forever.

Anwar Sadat (1918-81)

The ongoing conflict in the Middle East has claimed many lives, including Count Folke Bernadotte's (mentioned above), but two of the most dramatic and deliberate killings of high-profile figures have been those of Sadat and Yitzhak Rabin. On

6 October 1981, Egyptian President Sadat, along with a thousand guests, was attending a military parade in Cairo marking the anniversary of the 1973 Yom Kippur War. Part of the parade included a flyover of jet fighters trailing coloured smoke. While the crowd stared up at the sky, Islamic fundamentalists, who were part of the dangerous Al Jihad group, wearing Egyptian army uniforms — some were sleeper cells who had infiltrated the army, others were simply in disguise — pulled up in a truck on the parade ground in front of the audience stands. Suddenly, Hussein Abbas Mohammed, a sleeper and champion marksman in the Egyptian army, stood up on the top of the truck and fired at Sadat. Despite being 50 yards away, he was able to shoot Sadat in the neck. Then, First Lieutenant Khalid al-Islambouli, also a sleeper member of the group along with the marksman, began throwing hand grenades at the podium where Sadat sat, while the others provided cover fire. The First Lieutenant approached the podium and, from a few metres away, fired continually into the already heavily injured Sadat's body. At the end of the carnage, eleven people were killed (including Sadat) and twenty-eight more were wounded.

When Sadat signed a peace treaty with Israel in 1979, he essentially signed his own death warrant: many of his own people believed he had surrendered to Western pressure and betrayed the Arab cause. Sadat's lenient treatment of fundamentalism in his own country resulted in a steady growth in members of groups such as Al-Jihad, many of whom were infiltrated into Egypt's own armed forces, and his actions in 1979 gave them, in their eyes, just cause to eliminate him. In the immediate aftermath of Sadat's assassination, it appeared that the Islamic fundamentalists had not achieved their aim of causing a popular uprising among the Egyptian people, and very little changed in the state with the exception of the installation of a more merciless leader in Hosni Mubarak. Five of the men involved in the assassination were sentenced to death — military personnel Khalid al-Islambouli and Hussein Abbas Mohammed faced a firing squad, while two civilians and engineer Mohammed Abdel-Salam Farag, who was convicted of leading the plot, were hanged. While an Islamic state was not created and an uprising did not follow the assassination — a popular uprising of the people against Mubarak's authoritarian regime did not occur until as recently as 2011 — Sadat's assassination proved to Islamic extremists that a small group of people could affect the lives of many through terrorist warfare, a lesson they would continue to learn, up to the 2001 bombing of the World Trade Centre in New York, and beyond.

Yitzhak Rabin (1922-95)

The circumstances surrounding the assassination of Israeli Prime Minister Yitzhak Rabin, are often compared with those of John F. Kennedy: the public setting, the grainy video footage, the lone gunman and the conspiracy theories. Of course, the cheering crowds that greeted JFK as he drove through Dallas created a different atmosphere from the tension that bubbled in Tel Aviv, Israel, on the evening of 4 November 1995. A rally was in progress, organised in support of the peace agreement Rabin had reached with Palestinian leader Yasser Arafat, to try and give Palestinians self-rule in Gaza and the West Bank. Many Israelis were against the agreement, and staged violent protests vilifying Rabin, and the peace rally, held in Kings of Israel Square with more than 100,000 people, was an effort to counteract these demonstrations.

According to the official version of events, after Rabin made a powerful speech exclaiming the country's desire for peace, he made his way down from the stage, towards where his car was waiting. A twenty-five-year-old law student named Yigal Amir was waiting near the car. Despite not having any security clearance and being a known member of a group not shy about its desire to kill Rabin, he was not questioned by police. Approaching Rabin from behind, Amir stepped forward and fired. Security personnel descended on Amir, while bodyguards bundled Rabin into the car and tried to make the short journey through the crowds of people to the nearest hospital.

Rabin was dead an hour later. The whole catastrophe was captured on film by Roni Kempler, an amateur photographer who worked for the State Comptroller's office and was stationed with his video camera on the roof of a mall overlooking the crime scene. The footage opened up a can of conspiracy theory worms, as many believed ballistics evidence, combined with the video footage, proved Rabin had been shot from the front and that Amir had merely fired blanks. Although there is substantial evidence implicating others, Amir believed he had killed Rabin, and while never showing any remorse for his actions, believed that Jewish law granted him permission to take Rabin's life. He was sentenced to life in prison for his actions.

The royal death that started a war: Franz Ferdinand (1863-1914)

Victim

In life, Archduke Franz Ferdinand was the future of the Austro-Hungarian Empire, the heir to a throne that governed the second largest country in Europe at the time, and a number of different nationalities. But in death, he was the man whose demise created political scenarios that, in turn, led to the start of World War One.

As the nephew of Emperor Franz Joseph, he had become first in line to the throne after the shocking suicide of his cousin, Crown Prince Rupert, and his own father's death in 1896. He had also suffered the tragic loss of his aunt, Empress Elizabeth, who had been assassinated in 1898. The archduke was not particularly liked by his uncle, largely because of his controversial marriage to a Czech countess, Sophie Chotek. The Hapsburg establishment felt the countess' blood was not pure enough to be mixed into the family line and had tried to discourage the marriage. In 1900, after the death of his father and a few days before his wedding to Sophie, Franz Ferdinand took a humiliating oath in a Hapsburg court, vowing that his children would have no rights to the throne, and his wife would not receive the same privileges as him or be treated as royalty. Interestingly, the trip to Sarajevo in 1914 that cost the couple their lives, was the first time Sophie had been permitted to appear in public with her husband.

Assassination

The streets of Sarajevo were decorated with flags and flowers to mark the visit of the archduke, who arrived by train on the morning of 28 June 1914. The event had been widely publicised, and people lined Appel Quay, a wide avenue near the city's Miljacka River, eager to catch a glimpse of the royal couple. The convoy of seven cars included the mayor and the police commissioner in the first car, and, in the second car, which was open-topped, were the archduke, his wife and General Potoriek, the Governor of the Austrian provinces of Bosnia-Herzegovina. As the motorcade neared Cumurja Bridge, a man threw a metal object at the archduke's car, but it bounced off and exploded in the road, injuring some bystanders and Franz's personal secretary, Colonel Merizzi, who was a passenger in the third car. Franz Ferdinand was outraged by the attempt on his life, making it clear to the mayor when he tried to start his welcome speech a short while later at City Hall. 'I come here on a visit and get bombs thrown at me. It is outrageous.'

Clearly, despite the obvious risk to the archduke's life, everyone thought the worst was over, and the royal party had had a lucky escape. But the worst was yet to come. Probably insulted by the violent welcome the archduke had received, it was decided that the visit to the city would be cut short, and previously arranged engagements were cancelled. Before they returned to the train station, the archduke insisted on visiting Merizzi in hospital to check on his state. On the return journey down Appel Quay, the driver of the first car followed the original route rather than taking a turn towards the hospital. When General Potoriek realised this, he ordered the chauffeur of the archduke's car to turn around. By some horrible coincidence, one of the would-be assassins found himself standing a few feet from the car when it stopped. Seizing his chance, the man pulled out his gun and fired twice, hitting Franz Ferdinand in the neck and Sophie in the abdomen. After the shock and panic of the attack, the chauffeur drove to the governor's residence to seek medical attention, but Sophie was found to be dead on arrival, and the archduke joined her in death ten minutes later.

Assassins

At the final count, twenty-five people stood trial for the conspiracy and assassination of the archduke and his wife. It would emerge later that seven men had been stationed along Appel Quay at various intervals with the aim of killing the royal couple. Rather surprisingly, of the seven conspirators, only two were over the age of twenty. Six of the seven men were Bosnian Serbs, and one was a Bosnian Muslim named Muhamed Mehmedbasic. Mehmedbasic was the first man to watch the motorcade roll by without discharging a weapon, and he would claim that a policeman was standing too near to him to risk the attack. The seven men had spaced themselves out along the roadside, and the second in line who threw the bomb was Nedjilko Cabrinovic. Almost immediately after the explosion, the would-be assassin swallowed a cyanide capsule (all the conspirators carried these) and jumped into the shallow river. He was quickly retrieved by police since the cyanide was not strong enough to kill him. Other conspirators admitted to their inability to carry out the planned attack: nineteen-year-old Trifko Grabez wrote in a letter to his father that he was afraid to throw his bomb, as he knew it was likely innocent people would be hurt, while Vaso Gubrilovic, aged just seventeen, was nervous about hurting Sophie and so didn't fire his weapon. Gavrilo Princip was the 'lucky' man who found himself almost face to face with the target on the motorcade's return journey along the Quay. He also swallowed his cyanide capsule, which resulted in severe sickness but not the death he hoped for. He was arrested, along with his fellow conspirators, to face trial for the murder.

Motives

The Bosnian Serbs were part of a growing movement of Serbian nationalism, which saw the Southern Slavs encouraging the Serbian community, including those living in the northern territories, to unite through terrorism with the aim of creating a Greater Serbia. Serbia, the first nation-state in the region, was particularly resentful towards Austria-Hungary, which had annexed Serbian provinces Bosnia and Herzegovina in 1878. The visit to Sarajevo of a Hapsburg royal around the anniversary of Serbia's 1389 defeat by the Ottoman Empire in the Battle of Kosovo (when Serbia originally lost its independence), traditionally acknowledged as a day of mourning, was considered to be particularly confrontational to the Serbian nationalists. While Princip originally claimed to have acted alone in his plan, Cabrinovic's confession revealed the wider conspiracy and the involvement of the Serbian Comitaji, an offshoot of the Black Hand revolutionary organisation. Franz Ferdinand was assassinated not for something he did, or who he was, but for what he represented to the Serbian people. His murder was a violent act committed by young men eager to sacrifice themselves and the lives of others for the future of the Serbian people.

Aftermath

Because of the age of most of the defendants who had been stationed along Appel Quay on the day of the assassination, five were too young to receive the death penalty, and were sentenced to prison, receiving between thirteen and twenty years (twenty was the maximum prison penalty the judge could give). Princip and Cabrinovic both died from tuberculosis within a few years of their sentences beginning. It is widely believed that the assassination was organised by a senior intelligence office in the Serbian army named Colonel Dragutin Dimitrijevic, who was also involved in the Black Hand. A military trial for Dimitrijevic and three other Black Hand members was staged in Serbia, and all the men were condemned to death. Despite this trial, many believed the Serbian government had known about the assassination, and had these men executed so they could not reveal the truth of the state's involvement.

There was also speculation that the archduke's own family were behind his gruesome death. Unfavoured as heir, sending him to Sarajevo on such a provocative day of the year was like sending a lamb to the slaughter. The attack by Bosnian Serbs gave the Austro-Hungarian Empire the excuse it wanted to invade Serbia. With the support of their ally Germany, Austria-Hungary made fifteen demands of Serbia, which they would have to comply with if they wanted to avoid war. Serbia accepted most of the terms of the ultimatum with the exception of one that would allow Austrian police to operate within Serbia to investigate the assassination. Despite calls for diplomacy and peaceful reconciliation from across Europe, Austria-Hungary declared war on Serbia on 29 July 1914. Russia supported Serbia and prepared troops for war, while Germany declared war on Russia in retaliation and then on

Russia's ally France on 4 August, the same day Great Britain declared war on Germany. World War One had begun.

Assassinations fit for a king

The royal families of Europe were not that different from the Roman dynasties that inspired them. Wealthy heads of state who live off the taxes of the poor, and inherited titles, will always be a target for resentful citizens. But the illegitimate heirs, regent rulers and illicit affairs of royal families gone by, often meant the monarchs were not at risk so much from the general public as they were from members of their own family. As far as many of these plotters were concerned, there was nothing quite like an assassination carried out by a faithful servant to help steal money, titles and power from under a relative's cold, dead feet. Here we explore some of the royal family members who faced their end at the hands of an assassin.

Louis I, Duke of Orleans (1372-1407) and John II, Duke of Burgundy (1371-1419)

The Hundred Years' War waged between the royal houses of France and England over the French throne, resulted in the death of many a Frenchman. But the inner quarrels for influence and power over the future King of France led to the untimely deaths of these two noblemen, and the monarchy's instability meant much land was lost to foreign invaders during this period.

Louis I was the brother of the reigning king, Charles VI, while John II was Charles's first cousin. Charles suffered from psychotic episodes through much of his life, resulting in his uncle Philip (John's father) taking control over many of monarchical duties. Charles had a son who was heir to the throne, and after Philip's death, Louis and John fought to be the guardian of the dauphin and Charles's other children, even publicly threatening each other. Despite reconciling on 20 November 1407, when the two men shared communion together, three days later, Louis was ambushed and killed on Rue Vieille-du-Temple by a group of masked men; his left hand was chopped off and his brains were spilled onto the road. John would later publicly admit to orchestrating the assassination to rid France of a tyrant, and would eventually win back the king's favour.

But the rivalry was not over as Louis's son, Charles, formed an alliance through marriage with the Armagnacs, and soon John and the Burgundians were fighting a civil war against him. John even attacked Paris, forcing the dauphin to flee. He would later hold peace talks with the dauphin (the future Charles VII), the second of which took place on a bridge at Montereau on 11 September 1419. John had been warned that his life was in danger, but he strode out onto the bridge to meet the dauphin and his men. He would never return because Charles's companions attacked the duke, and, while the dauphin himself did not appear to give the order, the questionable accounts of that day mean the truth is still being debated.

Lord Darnley, Henry Stewart (1545-67)

Mary, Queen of Scots, was an unpopular ruler when she arrived in Scotland in 1561, after the death of her first husband King Francis II of France. As a Catholic in a predominantly Protestant country, she struggled to win favour at court and so married her Scottish cousin Henry Stewart, Lord Darnley, in an attempt to appease the nobility. In truth, she had formed an attachment to James Hepburn, the Earl of Bothwell, and once married and pregnant, she excluded Darnley from government, and her social life. Jealous and discontented with his lack of power and prominence, Darnley plotted with some of Mary's Protestant enemies, who conspired to assassinate her friend and Italian secretary David Rizzio, which they did.

There's no doubt this would have displeased and distressed the queen, but she was unable to divorce Darnley as it would render her new-born son (the future King James I of England and VI of Scotland) illegitimate. Bothwell, who was at large in government, invited leading exiled Protestants back into the country, and despite their past differences, there was an agreement between them that something had to be done about Darnley, although probably for different reasons. On the night of 1 February 1567, while the queen was attending a masquerade ball at Holyrood Palace, her husband was sleeping in an Edinburgh house. At 2 a.m., a gunpowder explosion demolished part of the building but, because Darnley's body and that of a servant were found on the lawn outside the house, he had clearly become aware of the plot and tried to escape from a window using a rope. Some accounts believe the men were killed by the force of the explosion and fell to their deaths, while others say they were strangled and stabbed by their assassins as they tried to flee. Bothwell's Protestant co-conspirators blamed the assassination on him, and the queen's reputation was also ruined. The two of them married and Mary abdicated the throne, but theirs was not to be a happily-ever-after romance. Mary was taken prisoner by the leading Scottish Protestants and Bothwell fled to Norway to evade capture. Mary, Queen of Scots, spent the rest of her life as a prisoner, and was executed twenty years after Darnley's death, under the orders of Queen Elizabeth I of England.

King Henri III of France (1551-89)

Despite the fact Henri's death marked the first murder of a French monarch and the end of the Valois dynasty, the assassination twenty-five years later of his successor, Henri IV, has been more widely studied and documented by historians.

The disappointing king, whose liberal attitude and fair hand were eclipsed by his apathetic approach to ruling, his effeminate dress and entourage of similarly clad 'Mignons' was attacked in his bedchamber by a fanatical Dominican monk named Jacques Clement. Clement managed to obtain an audience with the king on 1 August 1589 after travelling to Saint Cloud outside Paris, where Henri was stationed with an army. Under the pretence of having an important letter to deliver to the king, Clement handed him the paper and then stabbed him in the stomach. Rushing into the chamber, two of the king's men stabbed Clement and threw him out of a window to his death, but it was too late to save the king whose wound was beyond the help of contemporary medicine, and, despite the monarch despatching letters to his allies claiming he would recover, he died at 4 a.m. on 2 August.

King Henri IV of France (1553-1610)

Although Henri III, languishing on his death bed, had warned his heir about the dangers of one's own subjects turning against one, scholars believe that Henri IV may have been subject to up to twenty attempts on his life. Because of his own Protestant upbringing, he narrowly survived being killed years before he was crowned in the St Bartholomew's Day Massacre (1572), when leading French Protestants were attacked by Catholics: Henri renounced his faith to escape death. As king, he was popular, and attempted to bridge the hostile gap between the two factions, bringing peace to France for the first time in decades; but his Protestant roots were undeniable, and, to some, it was unthinkable that he had become king in the first place. On 14 May 1610, Henri, together with three of his courtiers, was being driven in his carriage through the streets of Paris to visit his finance minister who was sick and unable to attend court. En route, the carriage came to a halt, not unusual in the tiny crowded Parisian alleys, and a footman stepped down to see what the holdup was. Suddenly, a red-haired man emerged from the crowd, jumped up through the open window of the carriage and stabbed Henri in the chest. The assassin was a fanatical Catholic named François Ravaillac who was quickly apprehended by the crowd. By the time Henri's carriage made it back to the Louvre Palace, the king was dead. Many believed Ravaillac had acted as part of a Catholic conspiracy to kill the king, but he remained steadfast till the end that he had acted alone, because of Henri's lenient treatment of Protestants and a belief that the king would soon start a war with the Pope. His execution was particularly torturous: his limbs were stretched for hours before he died, after being drawn (disembowelled) and quartered (where a person's limbs are pulled in different directions by four horses, or their body is cut into four pieces).

King Gustav III of Sweden (1746-92)

Gustav was certainly not the most popular of Swedish kings. He reinstated absolute monarchy at the expense of the people and removed their civil rights, which had previously been extended to those beyond the nobility. He also frequently frittered away the country's money on things that he enjoyed, but it was to be his military policies that saw three men bring an end to his life. As a playwright and art lover, Gustav was Sweden's first real patron the arts, creating a number of artistic institutions and regularly attending operas, plays and concerts. On 16 March 1792, he was attending a masquerade ball at one such institution, the Royal Opera House. At dinner before the ball, he was handed an anonymous and threatening letter, but he had received such death threats before and so ignored it. At the ball, the three men, a captain in Gustav's army named Jacob Johan Anckarstrom, and two counts, easily located the king despite the masks, because of the silver star worn on his cape, a symbol of the Royal Order of the Seraphim. The two counts approached the king and complimented him on his mask while Anckarstrom shot him in the back with a pistol. They fled the opera house but were arrested the next day. The injury was severe but did not kill the king. He died nearly two weeks later when the wound became infected.

King Umberto I of Italy (1844-1900)

In May 1900, an Italian immigrant named Gaetano Bresci travelled from the United States back to Italy to join an anarchist group and assassinate King Umberto I. Bresci worked as a silk weaver in the US but put most of his energies into establishing an Italian anarchist newspaper in Patterson, New Jersey, because he harboured a deep-seated hatred of the Italian monarchy. On 29 July 1900, King Umberto attended a sporting competition to hand out prizes to the athletes. After the prize-giving was over, he retired to his carriage, which is when Bresci struck. He fired four shots at the carriage, hitting the king three times in the chest, killing him within seconds. Bresci received a life sentence for assassinating the king, but died under suspicious circumstances in his prison cell a year later. He made it clear in court that he had intended to kill Umberto to avenge the deaths of hundreds of Milanese protestors who had been shot at by soldiers under General Bava-Beccaris's orders as they approached the Royal Palace, demonstrating over rising food prices.

King Alexander I of Yugoslavia (1888-1934)

The death of Alexander I was one of the first public assassinations to be captured on film. The black and white video seen around the world was immensely shocking at the time, for the public rarely saw such violent and dramatic newsreel footage. The cameramen who experienced the catastrophe were filming the king's arrival in Marseilles for a state visit on 19 October 1934. He was there to discuss the possibility of a Franco-Yugoslav anti-Hitler alliance. The Kingdom of Yugoslavia existed during the tumultuous interwar years, and was formed from the states of Slovenes, Croats and Serbs and the Kingdoms of Montenegro and Serbia, after the end of World War One. The king's authoritarian rule, which had seen him abolish the parliament and outlaw religion to try and unify the various factions and cultures of the country, had made him unpopular. Alexander had been given an arrival befitting a king and was making his way by car through the city's streets, seated beside French foreign minister Louis Barthou, when a gunman leapt from the crowd and, before the police escort could stop him, stood on the car's running board and fired directly at the king. Alexander, Barthou and the chauffeur were all killed, so the car stopped instantly, allowing the cameras to keep filming the aftermath. The crowd descended on assassin Vlado Chernozemski, a Bulgarian member of a Macedonian revolutionary organisation, and beat him to death.

Chapter Three: Rights, Riots and Revolutionaries

I have a dream that one day this nation will rise up and live out the true meaning of its creed, 'We hold these truths to be self-evident, that all men are created equal'
Martin Luther King Jr.

Assassinations had traditionally been used as a method of power transference or political change. Less powerful groups and individuals eliminated those at the top, believing either it was their noble duty to overthrow tyrannical leaders, it was God's will or, simply, their time to sit on the throne. Of course, the change brought about this way by groups inferior in funds, size and military strength, can sometimes have a hugely detrimental effect on dynasties, politics and power, but more often than not, unwanted leaders are replaced by an heir or a willing supporter ready to step into their shoes; the angry mob remains angry, the lone assassin is captured or killed for the cause.

In other cases, violent measures and unwavering commitment see the burgeoning power of the few tip the scales to bring about change. The powerful become the powerless and, in the case of revolutionaries such as Jean-Paul Marat and Emiliano Zapata, their deaths are seen as the only way to break the will of their followers and restore the *status quo*. The loyal support and call to action some men and women have inspired in others can be a staggering and intimidating force to those who do not wish to see change, and believe strongly against the ideologies of revolutionaries and demonstrators. By silencing the loudest and most stirring voices of a minority movement, assassins hope to crush the spirit, delay progress or prevent change altogether. Of course, history keeps trying to teach these assassins that, if you destroy the loudest voice, you will only inspire the crowd to turn up the volume. A martyred leader can continue to bring change even after they are dead and buried, sometimes more effectively than when they were alive.

Jean-Paul Marat (1743-93)

Marat once wrote, 'To pretend to please everyone is mad, but to pretend to please everyone in a time of revolution is treason'. In the same way that Shakespeare's play *Julius Caesar* is responsible for many people's understanding of the dictator's end, the painting *The Death of Marat* by Jacques-Louis David has remained one of the defining images of its subject's death and the French Revolution. Of course, while the image depicts Marat with glowing white skin, reclining in a bath with a stab wound to his chest, his fingers still grasping the quill with which he wrote such stirring words to the people — a martyr for his cause — the truth of his death is a little different.

Victim

Born in Switzerland in 1743, Jean-Paul Marat studied medicine in France and, after working for nearly a decade in England, returned to France and worked as the doctor in the household of the king's brother. His time in England had introduced him to a more rhetorical, sarcastic and flamboyant style of journalism, which he began to pursue himself in 1789 when revolution first gripped the French people. Marat's self-published paper *L'Ami du Peuple* (*The People's Friend*) favoured the working classes and rallied them to arms, inciting mass executions of traitors of the revolution. In the spring before his assassination, he was an acting deputy in the National Convention and Secretary of the Committee of Surveillance, a body set up to expose anti-revolutionaries. Although his views and writings were not favoured by all the members of the Jacobin Club, he was declared president of the group in April 1793. Attempts made by the more right-wing Girondist group to remove him were unsuccessful. Marat was even arrested and tried for writings that claimed the Girondists were anti-revolutionary, but he was acquitted and was carried out of the court room by his supporters, who placed a laurel wreath on his head, the sign of a Roman victor.

Assassination

Marat's assassination took place in the evening of 13 July 1793. It was on this day when the French revolutionary received a visitor, a gentlewoman named Charlotte Corday. She had sought an audience with him at his home earlier in the day but was turned away, and so had sent a letter requesting he see her, to which she had received no reply. Insisting that she deliver another letter by hand, she returned to Marat's house and spoke loudly to his fiancée on the stairs about an important message she had to impart. Marat called out for her to be let in and she entered the room where he was seated in a bath. Marat suffered from a debilitating skin condition, which had left him somewhat disfigured, and towards the end of his life, he spent a large portion of the day submerged in a medicinal bath with a damp turban soaked in vinegar on his head. He had a board placed across the bath, so he could write while he was being relieved of his symptoms. Corday sat in a chair near to him and read out a list of eighteen Girondist deputies who were against the revolution in her hometown of Caen, people whom she actually supported. Then, suddenly, she stood up, pulled out a five-inch kitchen knife and stabbed Marat just above his collarbone (not a small injury below it as David's painting would suggest), puncturing his lung and severing a major artery. He died within minutes, but not before calling out to his fiancée, who rushed into the room. Corday did not make much of an attempt to get away and was apprehended by household staff and neighbours until the police arrived.

Assassin

Charlotte Corday was a young woman from Caen, a town in Normandy. As the daughter of a poor nobleman, she had received a formal education and was schooled in the history of Ancient Greece and Rome. Caen had become a centre for anti-Jacobin Girondist revolutionaries who had dominated the republican government and opposed Marat and what he stood for. In June 1793, the Jacobins seized power from the Girondists and arrested and guillotined many of the group's leading figures. Some had fled Paris and set up a new makeshift headquarters in Caen where they tried to rally support and organise a rebellion. No doubt Corday would have heard the speeches given by Girondist supporters that demonised Marat and painted him as responsible for the September Massacres when 1,400 Parisian prisoners awaiting trial, most suspected of being anti-revolutionaries, were beaten and slaughtered by frenzied mobs.

Motives

Corday's actions were heavily influenced by the Girondist speeches she had heard in Caen. While Marat claimed the Girondists were royalist supporters and defectors, they believed that he was polluting with a bloody dictatorship the republican ideal they were striving for. Corday was enamoured with the idea of a successful republic, as the Romans had strived for, and strongly identified her actions with those of Marcus Brutus because she was willing to sacrifice herself for the good of the people. She was very reasoned and logical in her approach to the assassination and her actions throughout, which emphasises how strongly she believed she was doing the right thing by taking Marat's life. Initially, she had planned to assassinate him in public at the National Convention where he was due to attend, but his illness prevented him from going, so the more intimate setting of his home became the venue. This plan, and her actions after she stabbed Marat, show how Corday had very little intention of escaping, and even at her trial she openly admitted, 'It is I who killed Marat… I killed one man to save a hundred thousand'. Corday stands out from most of the other assassins in this book. She was an educated woman with no previous history of violence or unusual behaviour, who saw her murderous actions as noble and self-sacrificing.

Aftermath

There was no doubt Corday had killed Marat, and if there had been, she quickly put it to rest by admitting her guilt at the beginning of her trial, which started four days after Marat's death and ended the same day. The pretty, articulate woman denied being in collusion with anyone else, and was sentenced to death. Her execution took place the same day as her trial and angry onlookers watched as Corday, dressed in a red shirt and with her hair cut short, stood upright in the cart that drove her to the guillotine, calm and collected. After she was beheaded, her executioner famously held up her head for the crowd and slapped it across the cheek, an act that was considered so disrespectful, the executioner was later tried and sentenced to twelve years in irons.

Both Marat's and Corday's deaths had significant impact on the people of France. Killing Marat did not bring an end to the bloody revolution, as Corday had hoped. If anything, it was fuel to the Jacobin fire which saw many more Girondist leaders, and thousands of others, guillotined. Marat was hailed as a martyr of the revolutionary cause by the Jacobins, and plans were quickly made for an elaborate funeral procession where his bathtub and bloodstained robes were carried behind his coffin to his resting place at the Pantheon. In place of the Catholic relics and icons the Jacobins had been swift to remove, they installed paintings and statues of Marat, the new saintly figure of France.

Emiliano Zapata (1879-1919)

Fighting for...

Zapata was a Mexican revolutionary who led a peasant army, known as the Zapatistas, in the early 1900s. The peasant uprising was initiated in 1910 by Francisco Madero, a presidential candidate who had lost against the country's tyrannical leader, Porfirio Diaz, and his call to revolution quickly spread to Mexico's provinces. While Diaz formally resigned in 1911, the country faced many years of fighting and hardship, as others struggled to take control of the country; even Madero was not able to go the distance, being assassinated not long into his presidency in 1913. Zapata, from the southern state of Morelos, led one of seven different armies and attempted to effect change in Mexico after 1910. He became a legendary and heroic figure in his part of the country, while Francisco 'Pancho' Villa was the north's equivalent. Zapata's plan, known as 'Plan de Ayala', was to take land from the rich estate owners' haciendas and distribute it to the working peasants in exchange for some compensation.

Wanted dead

By 1914, the Zapatistas, having survived many clashes with government forces and being considered a band of simple country folk, together with Villa's northern army, had occupied Mexico City and overthrown then sitting president Venustiano Carranza. But despite both Zapata and Villa's strong leadership skills, neither man wanted to form a government, and Zapata eventually returned home to Morelos to continue his struggle against the rich land owners. Carranza was officially elected as the new president in 1917, and soon realised that Zapata and his loyal supporters ruled the southern province that was rich in sugar cane farms and essential for Mexico's economy. The only way to win back the land was to kill Zapata.

The kill

It was 9 April 1919 when the revolutionary from Morelos was lured into a trap set by Carranza. Colonel Jesus Guajardo, a skilled cavalry officer in the federal army, was promising to defect and join Zapata's force. The two men agreed to meet, accompanied by thirty men each. Guajardo brought 600 troops with him, but still Zapata spoke with him and another meeting was arranged at a hacienda. The next day, Zapata rode into the estate's courtyard with ten of his men to meet Guajardo. A trumpet was sounded for their arrival and then the Colonel's troops raised their guns and fired a rain of bullets on Zapata and his men. The revolutionary's body was taken to a local police station for identification, and photographs were published around the world.

The legend of Zapata

While the rich rulers of Mexico considered Zapata to be an ignorant, brutish womaniser when he was alive, as the years went by after his death, he became a national symbol for Mexican people; a man who stood up for his beliefs and his community despite his lack of education, and who continued to fight until his end. Many believe Zapata rode into that courtyard knowing full well that his death was upon him but was prepared to sacrifice his life, believing it would strengthen the peasants' revolutionary cause. The stories, songs and films based on the lives of Zapata and Villa continue to inspire Mexicans living in poverty to this day.

Victim Villa

Zapata was not the only Mexican revolutionary to be assassinated in the early part of the twentieth century. Pancho Villa, whom Zapata had met for the first time outside Mexico City in December 1914, before the two men joined forces and occupied the city together, became a legend in his own right, after crossing the US border to attack the garrison town of Columbus, New Mexico and inciting 4,800 American soldiers to follow him back to Mexico and try and hunt him down. They were unsuccessful, and left the country defeated by the legendary general who was supported by the Mexican people's patriotism. By 1920, Villa had withdrawn from revolutionary life and spent most of his days living in the hacienda he had negotiated from the government, surrounded by fifty bodyguards. In July 1923, he attended the christening of one of his many godchildren in a village some fifty miles from his home. On the return journey, when his car slowed at a junction, gunmen who had been keeping watch for his return from an apartment near the road, opened fire and shot around forty bullets into the car. Nine hit Villa, killing him instantly, as well as his chauffeur and one of his assistants. Of the three bodyguards with him, two were fatally wounded. His assassins rode out of the garrison town, where soldiers were scarce, confident they wouldn't be attacked. The telegraph service was down immediately after the assassination, preventing more of Villa's bodyguards from tracking down the killers. Many believe the government was involved in Villa's death: they made little effort to investigate the killings and were satisfied when a man named Jesus Salas Barraza admitted to being the sole perpetrator of the crime. He served three months of a twenty-year prison sentence before being released with no questions asked.

Michael Collins (1890-1922)

Fighting for...

Collins was raised in a proud, nationalist farming family in southwest of Cork, Ireland. His father predicted on his deathbed that the then six-year-old Michael would do great things for Ireland. That nationalist spirit took hold of Collins as an adult and led him to be part of the failed Irish Easter Rising in 1916, where a disorganised Irish nationalist force attempted to seize a number of important buildings in Dublin, for which Collins was imprisoned. He was later elected to the Sinn Fein Executive and, in 1919, he became commander of the Irish Republican Army (IRA). Despite being involved in various deadly operations against British forces during the Irish War of Independence, Collins was a respected leader and was selected to be part of a delegation sent to Westminster to try and establish an Anglo-Irish treaty. The treaty effectively ended the war and allowed twenty-six of the country's thirty-two counties to be called the Irish Free State with complete control over their affairs, but with commonwealth status and allegiance to the king, while the six northern counties could opt in or out of the treaty.

Wanted dead

Collins signed the treaty on 6 December 1921, but without the crucial approval of President of the Republic, Éamon de Valera, who resigned after the treaty's ratification. Many people were unhappy with the terms regarding the partition of the country, but more importantly with the fact that the delegation had not insisted on republic status for Ireland. While it was approved by a small majority in the Irish Parliament, many hard line republicans felt Collins had betrayed the ideology they thought he stood for. By June of the following year, a civil war had begun over the terms of the treaty. On one side were the anti-treaty republicans and on the other, the pro-treaty Free State army, and in the middle was Collins, under pressure from the British government to restore order or risk the complete abolition of the treaty. This culminated in eight days of fighting in Dublin where Collins subjected the republicans to the full force of the Free State army, backed by ex-British and American soldiers, and they surrendered after sixty lives were lost. Collins had shown his support for the treaty and, in doing so, had essentially signed his own death warrant.

The kill

The county of Cork where Collins was born was also the setting for his death. On 22 August 1922, he travelled to Cork, against the advice of his security, to show his support for the victorious Free State army who had recaptured the city. As his convoy travelled down a country road near Clonakilty, a road block forced the cars to stop. Gunfire from the surrounding hills showered the convoy, and Collins immediately grabbed a rifle and began to defend himself against the attack. He was shot through the head and died at the scene — he was the only victim of the attack. Collins's assassin has never been officially named. In Dublin, hundreds of thousands of people watched as Collins's coffin was ceremoniously paraded through the streets to its final resting place in Glasnevin Cemetery.

The civil war did not end with Collins's death. If anything, the situation got a lot worse before it got better. Robberies, vandalism and murders were rampant and perpetuated by both sides of the cause. On 6 December 1922, one year exactly since Collins signed the treaty, the Irish Free State Government superseded the Irish Republic and the interim Government of Southern Ireland (of which Collins was chairman). This followed a period of intense hostility in which leading figures on both sides were executed. The IRA eventually resigned to dumping their weapons and admitting defeat and a ceasefire was agreed on 30 April 1923, which led to the imprisonment of around 13,000 republicans. In an election following the war, the Irish Free State was victorious, while de Valera would have to wait nine years before he regained power. The southern provinces of Ireland finally became a republic on 18 April 1949, but the hostility between civil war veterans who made up the majority of MPs would lead to problems in Irish politics for many years to come.

Ernst Röhm (1887-1934)

Fighting for...

As commander of the Sturmabteilung (SA, a paramilitary wing of the Nazi party), Röhm had been instrumental in the Nazi party's rise to power in the early 1930s, but, after seeing the phenomenal strength of the force he helped create grow to a point where it rivalled the German army, he began to entertain ideas of a 'second revolution' to take money and power away from the wealthy capitalist business owners, and to replace the army with the party-controlled SA. The SA were recruited from the pool of unemployed, angry young men the 1930s depression had left behind, and helped Adolf Hitler bully his way into power by beating up and intimidating those who opposed his National Socialist Party. By 1934, the SA boasted 2.5 million members, which alarmed leading army officials who saw the force's revolutionary ideology as a grave threat to Germany, and posed a risk of civil war. Röhm only saw possibilities and presented his plan for a 'People's Army' to the newly appointed Nazi cabinet members.

Wanted dead

To ensure his future control of and power over Germany, Hitler relied on the high-ranking officers and the business owners' financial backing. Hitler did not want a revolution, he wanted total control, and a revolution leading to a civil war was not part of his master plan. While Röhm was proposing the idea of revolution to the party, Hitler was plotting a campaign of 'moderation' to appease those whose support he now relied upon to progress and to eliminate the leaders of the very thugs who had helped him get this far. Röhm was at the top of his list and Heinrich Himmler's Schutzstaffel (SS) was the elite Nazi force preparing to kill those leaders and take the SA's place. When SS members held a demonstration in Munich opposing the Nazi regime on 29 June 1934, the threat of a revolution caused Hitler to act.

The kill

The day after the Munich demonstrations, 30 June 1934, would forever be known as the 'Night of the Long Knives'. Hitler had assembled all the leading SA members for a conference at the Hanslbauer Hotel in Bad Wiessee, near Munich. While they slept in the early hours of the morning, Hitler and his SS officers travelled to the hotel. At 6.30 a.m., Hitler stormed into Röhm's bedroom and, brandishing a whip, ordered that he be put under arrest. The number of people killed and arrested during this operation is widely disputed. Many believe about eighty-five people were killed by the SS, while over 100 more were arrested. Most of the victims of Hitler's purge were members of the SA, although leftist members of the Nazi party and a few senior army officials were also killed. Röhm was not assassinated that morning but taken to Stadelheim prison. A gun was left in his cell, as Hitler hoped he would kill himself. When he refused, two SS officers held guns to his bare chest and fired.

Problem solved

The revolutionary thorn in Hitler's side was gone. Without their experienced and passionate leader, the SA was no longer a force to be reckoned with in Nazi Germany. The Brown Shirts, as they were known because of their uniforms, continued to exist, although the force was greatly reduced; even more so after men were drafted for the World War Two effort, and with the rise of Hitler's SS, they ceased to be a threat to the party and its growing power.

Medgar, Malcolm and Martin: dying for rights in segregated America

The idea of having to petition for, protest about, and even fight for the rights so easily bestowed upon others simply because their skin colour is different from yours is a sickening and troublesome thought, but to be assassinated because you put your head above the parapet, spoke out and became a symbol of hope and possibility for those people is even more so. Medgar Evers, Malcolm X and Martin Luther King Jr. were all assassinated because of their outspoken views on the race and civil rights issues in the United States. Even though their views were not necessarily in line, their ability to charge a community, indeed a nation, with the words and the tools for change, made them heroic in the eyes of some, and dangerous in the eyes of others. Of course, these three men were not archaic kings taxing the people and raising the price of bread, they were not tyrannical dictators who would kill members of their own families to rule an empire and they were not corrupt politicians who had bombed countries, persecuted religious groups or restricted human rights. They were men of passion and ideas, whose oratory skills and refusal to back down in the face of adversity set them apart from the many others who felt just like them, and, as a result, made them key targets for those people wishing to slow the civil rights movement and silence the minority.

Medgar Evers (1925-63)

At twenty-nine-years-old, this Mississippi insurance salesman became the state's first field secretary for the National Association for the Advancement of Colored People (NAACP). Evers worked tirelessly on behalf of the state's African-American community through litigious and legislative means, to draw awareness to the civil rights situation and effect change. And his life's work was not without its successes: he was known for helping James Meredith, a young man who wanted to study at the University of Mississippi, but had been refused admission because of his race, to become the first African-American student at the institution. He was also noted for his investigative work, which saw him search for answers involving the murder case of Emmett Till, a fourteen-year-old boy from Chicago who was brutally attacked and killed in Mississippi, after allegedly grabbing a white woman by the waist and asking her on a date.

While Evers toiled away in Jackson, the state's capital, his position as a prominent black figure and investigator meant there were those who wished him harm and made a point of showing him so. He regularly received death threats and, a few weeks before his assassination, someone threw a bottle of gasoline into his garage, which did not explode.

The violence reached its peak on the night of 11 June 1963 when Evers, arriving home late from work, was shot in the back while getting out of his car. The assassin was hiding behind vine foliage and had attacked him with a hunting rifle. This was the same day President Kennedy had delivered a televised address on civil rights and outlined plans to give equal access to public schools to all Americans and to protect their voting rights. Evers's wife, who had fallen asleep watching TV waiting for him to come home, was awoken by three gun shots and rushed outside. Evers had crawled the short distance from the car to his doorstep, a trail of blood marking his path. He was taken to Jackson's University Hospital but died in the early hours of 12 June. Evers's death was a national news story — a first for the murder of an African-American in the US — and sparked demonstrations across the country. As a World War Two veteran, Evers was given a burial to mark the sacrifice he had made for his country at Arlington National Cemetery and over 4,000 people attended his funeral.

While the prime suspect in the assassination investigation was quickly linked to the killing, justice was a long way off for the Evers family. Byron de la Beckwith was a fertiliser salesman living in Mississippi, who was known for his hatred of the black community, as well as other minority groups in the state. The rifle used to kill Evers was discovered near to the crime scene with Beckwith's fingerprints on it, and he and his car were witnessed in the neighbourhood around the time of the attack, but he claimed his gun had been stolen, and the testimony of two policeman placed him 95 miles away from the attack at the time Evers was shot. While the case against him was strong, the two all-white juries that the defendant faced in 1963 and 1964 were split on the vote, and Beckwith walked free twice. It wasn't until 1994, some thirty years after Evers's assassination, that fresh evidence enabled prosecutors to bring a retrial against Beckwith. At seventy-three-years-old, he was found guilty by a multi-racial jury of the assassination. He served seven years in prison and died there at the age of eighty.

Malcolm X (1925-65)

Two years after Evers's death, a man named Malcolm X (born Malcolm Little) was shot at the Audubon Ballroom in Harlem, New York. Malcolm X had not lived the reputable and respected life of Medgar Evers, but, at the time of his death, he had found a new understanding and appreciation for life through Islam, and was working with the civil rights movement, campaigning for human rights for black Americans, and building international solidarity with black people from other nations.

Malcolm Little's parents were active members of the United Negro Improvement Association (UNIA), and he had grown up listening to his parents preach the separation of blacks and whites. The UNIA was different from other civil rights groups in that it promoted racial purity of the black community, and was often criticised for its likeness to the Ku Klux Klan. After a childhood of racist attacks, confusing ideologies and a lack of formal education, Little found himself in prison at the age of twenty-one for burglary. While there, he read widely and eventually came to learn of a new religious movement his family had become a part of, called the Nation of Islam. On leaving prison in 1953, he joined this faith led by Elijah Mohammed, which taught its followers that the first people were black and that white people were a devil race created by a troublesome black man who had been banished to an island for converting people away from the faith over 6,000 years ago.

Little devoted himself wholly to the religion at first (the 'X' replacing his last name was a sign of his conversion to the faith) and became a missionary for Mohammed, especially in

Harlem's Temple Number Seven where he preached. The Nation of Islam preached hatred of whites, supported violence against white domination and refused to support or trust black and white people, including Martin Luther King Jr., who were working hard for segregation to be eradicated. Malcolm X spent over ten years as a member of this religion before publicly denouncing it on 4 March 1964, after growing suspicious about Mohammed's authenticity and learning more about the real faith of Islam from some orthodox Muslims. In the last year of his life, he travelled extensively in the Middle East and Africa, most notably to Mecca to convert to Sunni Islam. On his return, he founded his own organisations, Muslim Mosque Incorporated and the Organization of Afro-American Unity, the latter of which promoted unity among disparate groups of African-Americans and their international brethren. It was precisely this withdrawal of support and complete turnaround from the Nation of Islam that led to Malcolm X's death.

The Audubon Ballroom was packed with people on the afternoon of 21 February 1965, eager to hear the famous Malcolm X speak. He had just begun when a man threw a smoke bomb near the back of the auditorium, then another jumped up from the front row and, with a sawn-off shotgun, fired twice at him. Reports differ, but it is believed two or three other men with revolvers fired at the preacher, their guns still going off as they attempted to escape from the hall. Fifteen minutes after the shooting, a doctor from the hospital across the street where Malcolm X was taken, announced to the crowd that he was dead. One man named Talmadge Hayer, a member of the Nation of Islam, was arrested at the scene and two more members of the religion were arrested later and received life sentences for the assassination.

While Malcolm X may not have lived a life like Evers, his funeral was attended by over a thousand people. His name and work continued to inspire those involved in the civil rights movement, and persuaded countless African-Americans to turn away from the racial hatred they were accustomed to and to be proud of who they were.

Martin Luther King Jr. (1929-68)

At about 6 p.m. on 4 April 1968, Martin Luther King Jr. left room 306 of the Lorraine Motel in Memphis, Tennessee and stepped out onto the balcony walkway. He was going out to have dinner with an old acquaintance, Reverend Samuel Kyles. The reverend had arrived in a chauffeur driven car to collect King and stood on the balcony with him. From the car park below, their driver suggested that King bring a coat with him because of the weather. King turned back into the room with the intention of asking his friend Reverend Ralph Abernathy to fetch his coat for him; there was a loud noise and then King fell to the floor. He had been shot in the jaw and the gaping wound was bleeding profusely. Police arrived on the scene, and King's friends and colleagues pointed across the street in the direction of a boarding house. An ambulance took King to St Joseph's Hospital, where doctors tried their best to save him, but the country's most famous civil rights advocate was dead — he had suffered brain damage and passed away at 7.05 p.m.

Martin Luther King Jr. was in Memphis to lead a march of striking workers at the request of Reverend Kyle. Famed for his involvement in the civil rights movement, King also campaigned tirelessly for America's poor people, and attended rallies and protests of striking unions and city workers who were being unfairly treated by the state. Despite being born into an America that tried to restrict the rights of African-Americans, King came from a fairly affluent family and received an impressive education, achieving a doctorate from Boston University. Raised by a Baptist preacher, he was a deeply religious man who believed passionately in addressing the inequality black people faced across the US, but especially in the South, which is where he became a pastor in Montgomery, Alabama, and eventually became an outspoken advocate for civil rights.

King was the president of the Southern Christian Leadership Conference (SCLC) which, together with organisations like the NAACP, supported the idea of peaceful protest and non-violent methods of instigating and influencing change. King's Christian beliefs informed his campaigning attitude and his oratory style, and he quickly became the face of the civil rights movement. When he, along with 250,000 others, marched in Washington, where he delivered his historical 'I have a dream' speech and achieved the media coup of the movement, he recognised that controversial marches, particularly in racist communities, brought more media attention to the cause.

Despite all the change he helped to bring about, there were many who wished King harm. Throughout his career, he received numerous death threats, and harassment by police and FBI agents. He was arrested and imprisoned, and was subjected to the violent reactions of those who opposed him — he was stabbed in the chest, punched in the face and his house was bombed. Many of King's enemies were white supremacists, but he was also losing favour with some members of the black community who were growing restless with his non-violent approach, and believed that physical action was the only real way to bring about change. On the evening before his assassination, he delivered a moving speech in which he sounded doubtful that he would live a long life. With the passion, poise and poignancy which, by that point, was expected of the preacher, he said, 'I am happy tonight. I am not worried about anything. I am not fearing any man. "Mine eyes have seen the glory of the coming of the Lord".' King was just thirty-nine-years-old when he died.

Who killed King?

On 10 March 1969, a man by the name of James Earl Ray was convicted of the assassination of Martin Luther King Jr. An escaped convict, Ray had rented a room at Bessie Brewer's boarding house across the street from the Lorraine Motel, at around the same time King checked in. His fingerprints were found on a hunting rifle left on the sidewalk outside the boarding house. Eyewitnesses said they had seen a man run from the building, drop the gun and drive off in a white Mustang. Detectives eventually tracked Ray down on 8 June at London's Heathrow Airport. He had travelled to Canada, Britain and Portugal in the time since King's death. In court, Ray pleaded guilty to King's murder, which meant he avoided the death penalty and a trial. Once sentenced, he changed his plea, claiming he had been set up and, while he had been present at the location with the gun, he had never shot King.

While Ray's story seemed a little implausible, there were many who believed that he didn't act alone in the plot. There were reports that members of the American Independent Party had offered sums of $20,000 and $50,000 to kill King, as well as rumours that other white supremacists had ordered the assassination. Many of King's family and associates, perhaps influenced by the FBI and CIA conspiracies surrounding JFK's murder, believe that the security services had something to do with his death.

Chapter Four: Tsars, Agents and Mystic Monks

There are no morals in politics; there is only expedience. A scoundrel may be of use to us just because he is a scoundrel
Vladimir Lenin

Old war paranoia and a string of Hollywood movies have done a lot to help paint the Russians as a nation of spies, assassins and power-hungry psychopaths. While these are clearly rather unfortunate stereotypes, there are a few real-life Russians who could give some of those Bond villains a run for their money. From tsars and holy men to politicians, journalists and spies themselves, there is a number of high-profile people who have fallen foul of, or come close to an untimely end at the hands of, Russian assassins.

Perhaps the most troubling of these tales are those that see secret agents, backed by government bodies, carrying out political murders. When an individual or a small minority group decide to kill a high-profile person, if they are not caught or killed at the scene, the authorities will endeavour to find them and bring them to justice. But with seemingly unlimited financial, technological and intelligence capabilities, and the backing of their country's government, assassinations carried out by elite forces and secret agents are often so carefully plotted, they don't appear to be assassinations at all, but rather accidental deaths, the result of natural causes or the fault of someone completely different. Some, however, such as the disturbing case of Alexander Litvinenko, come to the public's attention, often through being carried out carelessly, and cover-ups ensue, with government agents rarely facing thorough investigation, arrest or trial. The scope and power of agencies such as the Russian FSB or the American CIA have made state-sanctioned assassination an unchecked crime which has gone ahead, often without the knowledge or approval of senior officials or presidents.

From Russia with Love

Roman women were not the first to plot and scheme behind their husbands' backs, and they certainly weren't the last. Russia's Empress Catherine the Great (her real name was Sophia Augusta von Anhalt-Zerbst) earned her title by stealing the throne from her husband, Peter III, and seeing to it that he could not steal it back. As the son of Empress Elizabeth of Russia, Tsar Peter III was groomed for the throne from a young age and was married to Catherine when he was just fourteen. It was essential that they produce an heir to ensure the Romanov family line would continue. Rumours circulated in court that Peter was impotent and that he could not satisfy his new wife. Soon enough, however, Catherine gave birth to a son, Paul, a child many believed to have been fathered by one of her lovers. When Empress Elizabeth died, and Peter ascended the throne in 1761, Catherine's position in court and her son's future, were uncertain, and she feared her husband could send her into exile. Peter, however, was not a popular ruler and Catherine saw her chance to usurp him and gained military backing with the help of her lover, Count Grigorii Orlov. So it was that on 28 June 1762, Tsar Peter III of Russia was arrested and imprisoned while his wife was declared the new Empress. Rather than leave Peter to pose a threat from prison, Orlov, accompanied by his brother and some guards, rode to the castle where Peter was imprisoned. He sat drinking with Peter before strangling him to death. Catherine rewarded the Orlov brothers for their part in the assassination and she was crowned Empress that September.

Peter and Paul

Paul didn't learn much from his father Peter's unsuccessful reign and unnatural death. Rather than try and keep the court's favour, he sought to remove certain privileges from the nobility, and was more interested in improving the situation of the serfs and peasants. While these acts may have had good intentions, they ruffled a number of feathers, including those of his mother's last lover before her death, Count Platon Zubov. Zubov plotted with others, including the chief of police, to assassinate Paul. They broke into his bedchamber at night, attacked him with swords and then strangled him. Despite the fact the next Tsar was Paul's son, Alexander I, the assassins were never punished for their act.

Tsar Alexander II (1818-81)

Victim

Alexander II was the son of Nicholas I of Russia and his grandfather was Paul I. Alexander's father had ruled Russia with a tight fist. He restricted travel abroad, banned public meetings and made sure intellectuals knew their place by putting universities under police supervision. He even refused to allow people to smoke because he detested the smell of it. While he had tried to continue the work of his father by freeing the serfs, no real progress was made and peasant revolts continued. After Nicholas's death, Alexander set about the gargantuan task of ensuring that life would change for the peasants and serfs of Russia. After four years of trying, Alexander finally signed a document that would see many serfs receive a portion of the land on which they had worked, and most importantly, their emancipation.

Alexander also brought in a number of other significant reforms that liberalised education, introduced juries into the justice system, set up a ballot system for conscription that did not favour the upper classes and improved the country's infrastructure and financial institutions. But this radical improvement to the lives of the people was to be short-lived. Some of the changes did not considerably benefit the serfs, many of whom were no better off than before the new laws were introduced, and the students who had travelled abroad were filled with ideas of revolution and change. As unrest spread throughout the country, and Alexander began to fear for his life, the tsar tightened his control on his people and began to reintroduce old, oppressive laws which further rallied the people against him. A secret society of revolutionary and anarchic students, known as People's Will, believed that violent action was the answer to bringing about upheaval and political reform in Russia. They plotted to overthrow the tsarist rule of Russia by striking at its very heart and assassinating Alexander.

Assassination

People's Will was running out of time. The country was in turmoil, so Alexander made swift changes to ensure a more liberal policy was seen to be working, while simultaneously trying to sniff out the terrorists. The Secret Police were abolished and the press was given more freedom from censorship. As the people started to see the benefits of Alexander's new policies, they became less likely to rise up against the tsar, making it more difficult for People's Will to bring about a revolution. If that weren't a large enough spanner in the works, the police managed to arrest one of their members, who began to divulge their plans and secrets. And one of their leaders, Alexander Mikhailov, was arrested in October 1880. If they were ever going to have the chance to assassinate Alexander, this was it.

Every Sunday, the tsar travelled through St Petersburg to a riding academy where he reviewed the troops of the imperial guard. One of the assassin ringleaders, Andrei Zhelyabov, procured premises on the route the tsar would take through town in his carriage after visiting his troops. Under the guise of opening a basement cheese shop, the assassins were able to tunnel from the building directly under the road Alexander's carriage would travel on. They packed the tunnel space with explosives and made a form of hand grenade using the newly invented nitro-glycerine that two assassins would be ready to throw at the carriage if the plan went awry. When Zhelyabov was arrested in February, prior to the plan being carried out, the assassins knew they had to act fast.

On the day of the attack, the tsar's carriage took an unexpected route and it seemed that the assassins' plot had been foiled again, but the two hand-bomb attackers were not ready to miss their opportunity. One activist came forward from the crowds and hurled his homemade bomb at the carriage. It exploded and killed several people, but the tsar remained unharmed. Rather naively, thinking the attack had passed, he got out of the carriage to help those who were injured, and probably to be picked up by another carriage when the second activist tossed a vial of nitro-glycerine at his feet in what was clearly a suicide mission. Twenty men were killed in the explosion, including the assassin, and the tsar, while not killed on impact, had his legs blown off, his stomach blown open and he lost one of his eyes. He died shortly after.

Assassins

The People's Will was a splinter group from the former secret society Land and Liberty. Based in St Petersburg, Land and Liberty was a well-organised and widespread collection of individuals who aimed to bring about a revolution through violent methods. In 1879, the group dissolved into two parts: those who were against using violence to bring about change (known as Black Partition), and those who supported it (People's Will). The key players involved in Alexander's assassination were:

— **Ignatai Grinevitsky:** The second bomb-thrower, a Polish student who died in the explosion.

— **N. I. Kibalchich:** The explosives expert who stayed up all night to make sure the bombs were ready.

— **Sophia Perovskaya:** Andrei Zhelyabov's lover, in charge on the day of the assassination.

— **Nikolai Ryssakov:** The first activist to step forward and throw his bomb at the tsar's carriage.

— **Andrei Zhelyabov:** One of the group's leaders who arranged the cheese shop and tunnel digging before his arrest in February 1881.

All the conspirators, with the exception of Grinevitsky, survived the explosions. Ryssakov was arrested at the scene of the crime, and Perovskaya and Kibalchich soon after. These conspirators, along with their previous leaders, Mikhailov and Zhelyabov, were executed for the role they played in assassinating the Russian ruler.

Motive

While the tsar had made some moves to improve the rights of Russia's serfdom peasants and ordinary citizens, his reforms were not radical enough for those who wanted to see a constitution and fair representative government. Peaceful protest was not considered an option with the tsar's police force, and secret organisations such as People's Will, turned to violence in the hopes they could overthrow the regime and introduce a new, fairer government to their country. Inspired by revolutionary thinkers such as Louis-Auguste Blanqui and Mikhail Bakunin, and anarchic movements in parts of Europe, People's Will hoped that, despite their failed attempts in the past to educate the peasants about the possibilities of revolution, after assassinating Alexander, the peasants would take the opportunity to revolt and bring about change. Alexander might not have given the intellectuals everything they wanted, but he had introduced a number of new policies and practices, including involving locally elected representatives in some legislative decisions, despite the threats against him — it was time for the People's Will to act fast before the Russian populace became too comfortable with the tsar's reforms.

Aftermath

In one sense, People's Will had achieved its aim: the tsar was dead. But the fallout from this most public killing of the Russian leader was not what they had predicted. Other liberals, of the non-violent variety, were appalled at the terrorist actions of their contemporaries, and quickly saw their own attempts at reform halted under the new tsar. Alexander's son, Alexander III, saw to it that all those involved in his father's execution were arrested, charged and some sentenced to death for their involvement, which sent out a clear message to anyone thinking of plotting against the new tsar. Alexander III was arguably a worse option for Russia than his father as he was less interested in improving the lives of the people. While the country had been on the brink of introducing constitutional government, the tsar's death saw freedoms removed and restrictions reinstated, precisely what People's Will were hoping to eradicate.

Training to kill

Similar to a number of assassinations in this book, Alexander II's death was not the first time someone had tried to have him killed. The same faction of anarchists who eventual brought about his death, tried to assassinate him a number of times before they succeeded. Most famously, they had plotted to kill him when he travelled on a train across Russia in December 1879. Knowing that many people wanted him dead, Alexander travelled in a second train behind a decoy train. The plotters had learnt of this and planned to derail the second train by detonating an explosive charge on the railway. Their plan was a success and they managed to blow the second train off its tracks, then they realised that they were the ones who had been caught out — the tsar was travelling on the first train. Undeterred by their failure, a second attempt was made the following year when they planted a bomb in the banquet hall at the tsar's Winter Palace. The bomb exploded but the tsar and his family had not arrived and escaped unharmed. Unfortunately, when they decided to strike again in March 1881, he was not so lucky.

A night at the opera

Today, Piotr Stolypin is regarded as a controversial figure in Russian history, much as during his political reign. He was prime minister under Tsar Nicholas II and, while he helped launched important agricultural reform and brought some stability to the nation, he was known for not tolerating political opposition, and also for introducing faster prosecution methods, leading to swift executions. On 1 September 1911, he was in attendance at the Kiev City Theatre to see an opera. Tsar Nicholas and some of his family were also there. During the second intermission of the performance, Stolypin was standing near the orchestra pit, in conversation with some associates, when a man wearing a dress suit casually walked up to the prime minister, pulled a Browning revolver from his pocket and shot him twice, hitting him once in the hand and once in the chest. Stolypin would die from his injuries on 5 September. The assassin turned out to be Dmitry Bogrov, an anarchist who also worked for the secret police. In fact, it was the secret police who had given Bogrov a ticket to attend the opera because of a suspected assassination attempt on the life of the tsar. Some believed that Bogrov had acted on orders from the secret police to assassinate the prime minister, but this has never been proved.

Death of the 'mad monk'

When Grigori Rasputin's body was found in St Petersburg's Neva River on 18 December 1916, his lungs were filled with water, he had cyanide in his bloodstream and he had been badly beaten. There were also gunshot wounds to his shoulder, chest and head. The water in his lungs would indicate that, having survived a horrific, drawn-out assassination attempt, the Russian holy man had drowned. Rasputin's rise from peasant farms and religious sects to the Russian court, where he held the favour of Tsar Nicholas II's wife Alexandra and wielded political power, is even more fascinating than his dramatic and untimely death. Arriving in St Petersburg in 1903, the dishevelled 'mad monk' from Siberia appealed to the nobility's interest in alternative beliefs and spiritual practices. Despite being devoid of manners and formal education, he captivated the court, especially the women, who hung on his every word.

Alexandra became dependent on Rasputin, largely because of her belief that he could heal her son, the Tsarevich Alexis, who suffered from haemophilia, and this made it difficult for Nicholas to refuse him, even when the tsar's supporters believed Rasputin was undermining the royal family and making a mockery of their court. The effects of World War

One on the country resulted in an increase in national anger towards the Romanovs, so, in an effort to restore faith in the family, a number of Nicholas's allies, including his nephew-in-law Prince Felix Yusupov, his nephew Grand Duke Dmitri Pavlovich and Grand Duke Nikolai Mikhailovich, plotted to kill Rasputin.

On 16 December 1916, after coaxing him to Yusupov's riverside palace with the incentive of meeting Yusupov's glamorous wife, the plotters gave him cake and wine laced with cyanide, which failed to have any effect. Panicked, Yusupov shot him in the chest. But half an hour later, Rasputin opened his eyes and, being unguarded, he staggered from the palace. Out in the courtyard, right-wing politician Vladimir Purishkevich fired four more shots at him, two of which brought him to the ground. The assassins tied his hands and feet, wrapped his body in a curtain and, forgetting the all-important weights to stop his body from floating, tossed him in the river. When he was found by workmen crossing the river two days later, he was wearing a blue shirt embroidered by Tsarina Alexandra.

They may have been able to stop Rasputin, but the monk's assassins could not stave off the revolution. In 1919, the Bolshevik revolutionaries executed Mikhailovich for being a grand duke, and Purishkevich died while fighting against them in the civil war. Yusupov fled Russia, while Tsarina Alexandra exacted some revenge on Pavlovich by exiling him to Persia.

End of a dynasty

Rasputin's death did very little to assuage the Russian people's negative opinions of the Romanov family. Nicholas stood by his wife and family through the revolutionary uprising of 1917 and, probably with some relief, abdicated that year, marking the end of the dynasty's 300 years of Romanov rule. No longer in power or a threat to the Bolshevik revolutionaries, it seemed that Nicholas, his wife Alexandra and their five children, would be able to live out their lives in relative peace and contentment, but this was not the case. The tsar represented the old regime that the Bolsheviks had rallied to fight so hard to abolish. Confined to a palace near St Petersburg by the provisional government, surrounded by much of the splendour they had become accustomed to, the family was a sour reminder of the inequalities Russia had withstood for so many years. They were even offered an invitation from Nicolas's cousin King George V, to seek refuge in England, but some on the political left, both in Russia and in Britain, believed that this fate was too lenient, and the invitation was withdrawn.

After spending some time in the palace, and then being relocated to a former governor's residence in Siberia, the Romanov family were finally seized by a group of Bolsheviks and detained in a house in Yekaterinburg in central Russia in April 1918, where their daily lives changed dramatically under the watchful eyes of Yakov Yurovsky of the Bolshevik secret police. They had little privacy and were shut in their rooms at all times except to eat. Whilst some Bolsheviks had previously wanted to see the tsar put on trial, to expose the family's crimes in court as the civil war progressed, the Bolshevik leadership was soon more concerned about the anti-revolutionary army (White Forces) seizing Nicholas from Yekaterinburg and using him to increase support to their cause. As the Whites approached Yekaterinburg, the family's captors sent a telegram to Bolshevik leader Vladimir Lenin, informing him that Nicholas needed to be executed immediately and to send a reply if he disagreed. No reply came, and on 16 July

1918, nine days before the Whites took control of the city, the Romanov family was executed.

The family was woken in the middle of the night and told to dress and go down into the cellar for their own safety from the fighting taking place in the city. The family of seven were accompanied by their son's doctor and three servants — there were to be no witnesses. Once they were settled in the basement, eleven executioners — one for each person in the room — entered the small room and began firing chaotically at the family. When the smoke from the guns cleared, almost all of the family were dead. Young Alexis was still alive, so Yurovsky shot him again at point-blank range. The bodies were taken away and hidden in a mine shaft, before being removed and buried in a shallow grave. In 1991, a burial site believed to be the last resting place of the Romanovs, was excavated, and DNA analysis proved the bodies found were indeed members of the famous family.

Did they all die?

The secrecy and conspiracy surrounding the death of the Romanov family, and the lack of public knowledge of the family's burial ground, led many people to believe that there were members of Russian royalty who had survived the killing, especially the tsar's youngest daughter, Anastasia. One reason often given for the Grand Duchess surviving the shooting was the fact she had sewn diamonds on the inside of her dress, and they took the full force of the bullets. These rumours were compounded by a number of women who claimed to be Anastasia later in life, the most notorious of whom was Anna Anderson, a Berlin mental hospital patient who received much publicity after declaring she was the Grand Duchess. Her claims were widely believed, despite family members and those who had known Anastasia refuting them. DNA analysis was conducted on a lock of Anna's hair upon her death, which revealed she was not genetically connected to the Russian royals. The 1991 excavation of the mass grave of the Romanovs revealed two of the children's bodies to be missing, Alexis's and one of the daughters, either Maria or Anastasia. In 2007, two bodies were dug up in the Ural Mountains near Yekaterinburg, and a year later, DNA analysis proved they were the remains of the two missing Romanov children, finally concluding that the entire family had indeed died on 16 July 1918.

Lucky escape: Vladimir Lenin (1870-1924)

In August 1918, the same year that the Romanov family had been killed, someone tried to take the life of Vladimir Lenin, the leader of the Bolsheviks and the man who had helped bring revolution to the Russian people. Not everyone was happy with the Bolsheviks being in power, and many felt that revolution could be achieved by other means. Unfortunately, anyone who was seen to openly disagree with the party line was descended upon by the secret police, known as the Cheka, which only made the dissidents revolt further against Lenin and his Bolsheviks.

On the day Lenin cheated death, another man was not so lucky. Moisei Uritsky, the head of the Cheka, was assassinated in St Petersburg on the orders of the Socialist Revolutionary Party (a party that opposed the Bolsheviks), but Lenin went ahead and made plans to visit a factory outside Moscow to deliver a speech to the workers, despite the obvious risk to his life. After delivering the speech, Lenin left the factory and was making his way to his car when a group of women stepped forward to ask him some questions. One of them, Fanya

Kaplan, pulled a gun from her bag and fired it three times, hitting Lenin twice. He was immediately rushed to the Kremlin, while she was apprehended at the scene. She was executed four days later. When she was in custody, she confessed to having shot Lenin on her own without any assistance, and that she had resolved to kill him because he was a traitor to the revolution. Kaplan supported the Socialist Revolutionary Party, and had previously served eleven years hard labour in the Siberian salt mines for her involvement in a 1906 attempt to assassinate the governor general of Kiev.

Doctors decided not to remove the two bullets from Lenin's body — one was in his neck, the other in his lung — and he faced a slow and lengthy recovery. While Lenin did not die that day, the impact of the two wounds no doubt contributed to the forty-eight-year-old man's deteriorating health over the next few years. He would eventually die, following a number of strokes, in 1924.

Leon Trotsky (1879-1940)

Victim

Born in the Ukraine in 1879, to hard-working Jewish farming parents, Trotsky would go on to be one of the most significant Russians of the twentieth century. Unlike his illiterate father, Trotsky was educated from a young age and developed a remarkable gift for languages; he went on to complete school and attend the University of Odessa, being awarded a degree in mathematics. More influentially, during his time there, he learnt about the Revolutionary Movement and returned to the town of Nikolayev, where he had completed his secondary education, to start up one of the first trade unions. For instigating revolution, the young Trotsky spent time in prison, was exiled to Siberia and eventually found his way to Europe where he met Lenin in London for the first time. While the two men disagreed on many things, and Trotsky often spoke out against Lenin, they both favoured a more socialist Russia and found much common ground — they both struggled together to overthrow the tsarist regime and played pivotal roles in the 1905 and 1917 revolutions. Trotsky could be as ruthless as he was intelligent, needlessly slaughtering sailors at Kronstadt, who tried to revolt against the Bolshevik regime, and enforcing state control over the working classes after World War One, to try and stabilise the country. When Lenin died in 1924, a power struggle between the ambitious Josef Stalin and Trotsky ensued which resulted in the latter being exiled from his homeland in 1929, and the former becoming a dictator. As brutal and controlling as Stalin was, it would take him eleven years to have his rival murdered in Mexico, where Trotsky lived from 1937 until his death in 1940.

Assassination

Trotsky knew he was a wanted man, and that Stalin's powers stretched far beyond Russia's borders. Even in his Mexican fortress with its guard watchtower and constant police security, Trotsky wouldn't have felt safe. Things had come to a head in May 1940, after a failed assassination attempt had left the family's home riddled with bullet holes. A few days after surviving the attack, Trotsky met Ramon Mercader for the first time. Trotsky and his security detail were familiar with seeing Mercader around the complex, when he came to pick up and drop off his girlfriend who worked as a secretary there. Mercader was intelligent and, like Trotsky, could speak a number of languages. The two men spoke numerous times when Mercader was at the house over those three months, without Trotsky being aware he was an agent for the NKVD (People's Commissariat for Internal Affairs), who had been assigned to assassinate Trotsky. On 20 August 1940, Mercader brought an article to the house for Trotsky to read and as he sat at his desk perusing it, the assassin plunged an ice pick into his skull, causing Trotsky to scream in pain. Despite the injury, he managed to bite his assailant in the hand, forcing Mercader to drop the weapon, and make his way out into the corridor to call for help. Immediately, the security guards arrived and tackled Mercader to the ground. The two men were taken to hospital where, a day later, Trotsky succumbed to his wounds and died.

Failed attack

The attack on Trotsky, while surprising, was not a total shock. On 23 May less than three months before the assassination, his Mexican home had been riddled with bullets by a group of men carrying machine guns, and dressed in police and soldiers' uniforms. Despite the house being guarded by Mexican police, the intruders — a mobile group of the NKVD comprising twenty men, led by Mexican painter and member of the Mexican Communist Party, David Alfaro Siquerios, who had fought in the Spanish Civil War — were able to overcome them, tie them up, disable the alarm linked to the police station and cut Trotsky's phone line. The men then fired a rain of bullets at the Russian revolutionary's house from the courtyard. Seventy-six bullets would later be found in the walls and floors of the house.

At home at the time, Trotsky and his wife had crouched on the floor while the attack took place. Trotsky's grandson in another room was hit in the toe, but all three survived. The assassins had also left a bomb to finish the job, but it failed to go off. After the attack, Trotsky ensured that his home was fortified stronger than ever, but better security systems and more barbed wire would fail to be a match for the undercover assassin who ended Trotsky's life by being invited into his home.

Assassin

On the day he killed Trotsky, Ramon Mercader was more than prepared to carry out the orders he had received from NKVD operative Leonid Eitingon. He carried an ice pick and a gun in his pockets, and a dagger was sewn into the lining of his coat in case the other two weapons were discovered. It is likely that Eitingon selected Mercader for the mission because of his photographic memory, athleticism, language skills and intelligence. It was essential for Mercader to gain Trotsky's trust and not arouse the suspicions of the guards and other people at the house if he was going to be successful in eliminating Trotsky. After persuading his mistress, a Trotsky supporter, to move to Mexico City in January 1940 and take a secretarial job working for the Russian exile, Mercader was able to gain access to the complex and earn the trust of those who worked there. After his mistress left for New York, he continued to visit the Trotsky home. His mission, initially, was to provide intelligence to the mobile unit assigned with carrying out the assassination, but after they were unsuccessful, his directives changed and he planned his attack.

Motive

By the time Mercader plunged the ice pick into Trotsky's skull, the latter had been living in exile for eleven years. He had travelled from Turkey to France, to Norway and eventually to Mexico, where he settled in 1937. Although he had continued to produce writings and keep the anti-Stalin campaign alive with the help of his son Lev Sedov, living in exile so far from most of his supporters meant his power and grip on the people faded. Stalin, in contrast, was eliminating his political enemies left, right and centre. Almost all of Trotsky's family committed suicide or were murdered under Stalin's orders, and other Bolshevik revolutionaries, whom Stalin believed were conspiring with Trotsky to assassinate him, were also executed. In 1939, when the All-Union Communist Party met, with the exception of the exiled Trotsky, Stalin was the only member left of Lenin's original Politburo. And that seems to be largely the motive behind Trotsky's assassination: he posed a threat, however small, to Stalin's dictatorial rule.

Aftermath

Two premeditated attacks on Trotsky, carried out by professional killers, were flashing red lights to the authorities that organised units, most likely under orders from the NKVD, were behind the attempted and successful assassinations. That Stalin's hand could reach a Russian exile in Mexico sent a clear message to any Trotsky supporters or Stalin dissenters to toe the line. Mercader, arrested at the scene of the crime, was sentenced to twenty years in a Mexican prison. Despite offers to reduce his sentence if he admitted to NKVD involvement in the assassination plot, Mercader refused to reveal the true nature of his crime, staying loyal to his compatriots and remaining in prison until 1960, when he was released and returned to Russia.

The ice pick that killed Trotsky

In 2005, sixty-five years after Mercader's arrest, the mountaineering tool he used to bring about Trotsky's death apparently resurfaced, after having gone missing for over half a century. While others had claimed to have found the weapon in the past, this ice pick, complete with old blood stains, was in the possession of Ana Alicia Salas, the granddaughter of a secret policeman who worked on Trotsky's murder case in Mexico City. Trotsky's grandson, Sev Volkov, who had survived the first assassination attempt on his grandfather, ranthe Trotsky Museum from the Mexico City house the Soviet revolutionary was attacked in. He was willing to provide a DNA sample to test the blood on the axe, to see if it was the murder weapon, only if Salas was willing to donate the weapon to the museum.

Trotsky's death didn't sound the death knell for Trotskyism, but, without its leader, the movement failed to regain a strong enough voice to challenge Stalin, who proved more popular after his successful military leadership of Russia against Germany in World War Two. The war changed the face of Europe and European politics, so it's likely, with or without

Trotsky's assassination, the Communist Russia he and Lenin had both worked for would not have been achieved.

NKVD — the KGB's big brother

Before the KGB (The Committee of State Security) was officially established in Russia in 1954, the organisation went by the names Cheka and OGPU (United State Political Administration) and then NKVD (People's Commissariat for Internal Affairs) from 1934, the organisation behind Trotsky's assassination. The NKVD answered directly to Stalin, and he used the organisation for personal means to eliminate enemies, real and imagined, to imprison dissenters and to infiltrate Soviet society with fear and paranoia. A number of other high-profile Russians fell at the hands of NKVD agents, most likely under Stalin's direct orders.

— **Sergei Kirov:** As the leader of the Communist Party in Leningrad, Kirov was a powerful man and his more moderate approach to change posed a great threat to the more extremist views of Stalin. On 1 December 1934, as he was leaving his office at the party headquarters, he was shot in the back of the neck. The gunman, Leonid Nikolayev, claimed he was a successor of Tsar Alexander II's assassins, and appeared to be mentally unstable. He was arrested, tried and executed shortly after the attack, but when asked by Stalin, who came and visited the body of his former rival, why he had killed Kirov, he pointed at the NKVD officers in the room and suggested that the dictator ask them instead. Whether or not he was in on the plot, Stalin used Kirov's death as an excuse to root out other 'suspect elements' within the party and, with the NKVD's assistance, carry out the purges known as the Great Terror.

— **Ignace Poretsky:** Trotsky might have been far from Russia in Mexico, but the NKVD's arms were far-reaching, and others living outside the country were not safe from the various mobile groups designated to seeking out Trotsky's supporters, and burying them. Ignace Poretsky had previously been a spy for NKVD, but after the purges began, he sent a letter to Stalin informing him he was defecting and would not reveal any state secrets. Hiding in Switzerland with his family, he was persuaded to attend a meeting with Gertrude Schildbach, a family friend who had been recruited by the NKVD to give Poretsky a box of chocolates laced with poison. He attended the meeting but, at the last minute, she backed out. Poretsky's body was later found at the side of the road, full of bullet holes. In his hand was a clump of Schildbach's greying hair — he had used her body as a shield from the assassin's fire.

— **Lev Sedov:** Like the majority of Trotsky's family, his son was to meet a miserable fate, apparently having also been assassinated. Two and a half years before his father's death, the thirty-two-year-old came down with appendicitis and was told by his close friend, Mark Zborowski, to attend a private clinic run by exiled Russians. Zborowski was a trusted confidant of Sedov, but was, in fact, an NKVD agent. It's believed that Zborowski informed the NKVD of Sedov's destination and his appendicitis diagnosis. Trotsky's son received surgery at the clinic, but days after the operation on 13 February 1938, he began to feel ill again, and, after suffering for three days, he died. His wife believed he had been poisoned, and while evidence proved inconclusive, it is highly likely that at the clinic staffed by Russian exiles, where a number of NKVD agents were already working undercover, some foul play took place.

— **Rudolph Klement:** The headless body of another Trotsky supporter was found in the River Seine in July 1938. The body's scarred hands enabled friends to identify it as that of Rudolph Klement, the man Trotsky had tasked with organising the Fourth International revolutionary meeting later in the year. He had been missing from his home in Paris since 13 July.

Alexander Litvinenko (1962-2006)

The international media hysteria surrounding the shocking assassination of Alexander Litvinenko in 2006 told of clandestine meetings, Russian agents, poisonous substances and wicked deceit. A story that could have been straight out of a thrilling spy novel. But the final images of Litvinenko before he died: bald, frail and defeated, in a hospital bed, were an all-too-real reminder of the slow and painful end that the Soviet defector experienced. It was only after his death that doctors and investigators would learn what killed him and try to bring those involved in his death to justice. Sadly, despite more than five years passing since he died (at the time of writing), no one has stood trial for Litvinenko's assassination.

Victim

Born in 1962 in the city of Voronezh in south-west Russia, Litvinenko joined the Soviet military straight out of school, and later switched to the Secret Service agency, the KGB, in 1988, where he worked in the counter-intelligence department. In 1991, the KGB was renamed the Federal Counterintelligence Service (FSK), and then was reorganised under a new law in 1995, to its current name of the Federal Security Service (FSB). Litvinenko was promoted to the rank of lieutenant-colonel in the FSB's Organised Crime Control Directorate, which oversaw investigations into organised crimes and terrorist activities. But, in 1998, he broke from the secretive traditions of Russia's security services by organising a monumental press conference that aired on national TV, the ramifications of which would be felt only eight years later. At the press conference, Litvinenko, seated beside other Secret

Service agents wearing black balaclavas, accused the FSB leaders of corruption, running extortion rackets and ordering murders. He specifically claimed that they had ordered him to assassinate wealthy Russian businessman Boris Berezovsky. The dissenters were quickly silenced and Litvinenko spent time in prison for 'exceeding his official powers and causing bodily harm to witnesses'. After being released on the condition he would not leave Moscow, Litvinenko fled to the UK where he sought and was granted asylum. He lived in London until his death in 2006.

Assassination

On 1 November 2006, Alexander Litvinenko went to the Millennium Hotel in Grosvenor Square, to meet a business associate named Andrei Lugovoy who was staying there with his family and colleague, Vyacheslav Sokolenko. When Litvinenko arrived at Lugovoy's hotel room, Sokolenko was not there — he had taken Lugovoy's family sightseeing — but there was another unnamed man in the room, whom he did not recognise. Lugovoy introduced him as another Russian businessman, and Litvinenko thought nothing of it. Litvinenko drank some tea while they discussed business related to buying copper and liquidised gas at low prices and exporting them to Latin American countries for a considerable profit. He then left the hotel to meet an Italian friend, Mario Scaramella, for sushi, before returning to the hotel's Pine Bar later, only to find Lugovoy drinking with a Russian man already known to Litvinenko as one of Lugovoy's business connections, Dmitry Kovtun. They gestured to a cold green tea for the teetotal Litvinenko, but he declined it and ordered a fresh pot. Litvinenko then headed home to have dinner with his wife and son. Later that evening, he started to feel ill and spent the night vomiting. On 4 November, after three days of this mystery illness, Litvinenko was admitted to hospital in north London. As his condition worsened, he was moved to University College Hospital in central London, where his deteriorating condition was being treated as a potential poisoning case. He was placed under armed guard. After suffering dramatic weight loss and hair loss, and enduring extreme pain, on 22 November he had a severe heart attack and died the next day. As the case of Litvinenko has never been brought before a court, it has not been officially established precisely when Litvinenko ingested the poison that killed him. The former KGB man did meet with Lugovoy and Kovtun a couple of weeks earlier in October, when it is possible that a first attempt, or perhaps a practice run, was made to assassinate him.

What killed Litvinenko?

On 19 November 2006, it was reported that Litvinenko had been poisoned with thallium, a chemical used to kill rats. This theory was developed a few days later when toxicologist Professor John Henry said he believed that radioactive thallium may have been the cause. Litvinenko's doctors agreed it was unlikely that ordinary thallium would have caused the Russian's symptoms. On the day Litvinenko suffered a heart attack, thallium was ruled out as the cause by the hospital's director of critical care, Dr Geoff Bellingan. Three hours before Litvinenko's death, a special Ministry of Defence-governed laboratory, the Atomic Weapons Establishment, discovered what was killing him: a radioactive substance, believed to be polonium-210.

It is a highly radioactive and chemically toxic element. It is a risk to the human body only if it is absorbed through eating or drinking contaminated food or fluids, inhaling contaminated air, through an open wound or by ingesting or inhaling a contaminated person's bodily fluids. Tests were carried out at various locations in London where Litvinenko and his associates had been, and traces of polonium-210 were found at a number of them, including the hotel suite and bar of the Millennium Hotel, the sushi restaurant where Litvinenko had met Scaramella, and where he had met the Russian associates weeks before. The substance was also found on a number of aeroplanes, and a trail of polonium-210 took investigators to other European cities and to Russia, where they believed the poisonous liquid had been sourced. After a public warning was issued about the locations where polonium-210 had been detected, by 4 December, 3,000 people called a National Health Service helpline to seek information. Many were tested and a number of people tested positive for traces of polonium-210 in their bodies, including staff at the Pine Bar and police officers involved closely in the case.

Assassins

While no one has been convicted of assassinating Alexander Litvinenko, lengthy investigations have led British police to conclusions of who was to blame. On 22 May 2007, the Crown Prosecution Service, after assessing the evidence, said Andrei Lugovoy should be charged with Litvinenko's murder. Lugovoy, a former KGB agent, has never faced trial because the Russian government refused to extradite him to Britain. Professor of Environmental Toxicology at Middlesex University, Nick Priest, stated that before the poison reached London it would have been divided between four people and recombined in the hotel room. Despite this, no suspects have been charged. Two weeks before the meeting with Litvinenko, Lugovoy, who visited London six times in 2006, and Kovtun had travelled to London and checked into the Shaftesbury Hotel, had a meeting with Litvinenko at sushi restaurant Itsu, and then switched to the Parkes Hotel the next day. Traces of polonium-210 were found at all of these locations. Lugovoy continued to claim his innocence, saying he was a scapegoat for the assassination. He even claimed that British Special Services were involved in Litvinenko's death.

Motives

Litvinenko was clearly seen as a threat to the Russian President Vladimir Putin and the FSB. His years of experience and classified knowledge of the inner workings of the Secret Service, and his willingness to put himself at risk to tell the world about what he knew and what he believed was going on, made him a public nuisance to a number of high-profile Russians. From London, he wrote a number of articles published in the Chechen press, expressing his outrage at the atrocities being committed against Chechen civilians in the name of war, and he authored two books attacking President Putin, his government and the FSB. Litvinenko openly laid the blame on Putin for the 1999 apartment bombings in Moscow (which were blamed on Chechen rebels), and the 2006 killing of Russian investigative journalist Anna Politkovskaya, who had fearlessly exposed many of the war's atrocities. It is believed that, at the time he was poisoned, Litvinenko was investigating Politkovskaya's murder: she was shot dead in the elevator of her Moscow apartment building on 7 October, less than two months before he died, and she had previously survived a poison attempt herself. Whoever killed Litvinenko gave Putin's opponents a clear message: despite living what many would consider to be a safe distance from the Kremlin, you can run, but you can't hide.

Aftermath

Litvinenko's funeral took place on 7 December 2006. His body was buried at Highgate Cemetery inside a special, sealed casket that had been provided by the authorities, as his body still presented an environmental hazard. A statement by Litvinenko, which he composed two days before his death, spoke directly to Putin. 'You may succeed in silencing one man,' it read, 'but a howl of protest from around the world will reverberate, Mr Putin, in your ears for the rest of your life'.

British police travelled to Russia as part of their investigation, and Russian detectives travelled to London to interview witnesses and carry out their own inquiry. Ultimately, though, with Moscow refusing to extradite Lugovoy, the investigation was fruitless. As punishment for Russia's lack of cooperation, four Russian diplomats were expelled from the embassy in London; and in retaliation, four British embassy staff in Moscow were asked to leave, so damaging relations between the two countries. Lugovoy himself became a MP for the Liberal Democratic Party of Russia when he was elected to the State Duma in December 2007.

By the state for the States

Of course, Russia's KGB and FSB are not the only government agencies to get their hands dirty and use top-level intelligence to inform, aid or influence the assassination of a spy or foreign leader. The 1975 Church Committee was a select committee set up in the United States to investigate the illegality of intelligence gathering activities undertaken by the FBI and CIA during the 1970s. While it was the events of the Watergate scandal during President Nixon's time in office that sparked the committee's formation, the detailed examination of these security agencies revealed their knowledge and involvement of a number of assassination plots, attempts and executions. Most notoriously, between 1960 and 1965, the CIA, largely under President Kennedy, devised a number of plans to try and discredit, overthrow and even kill Cuban Prime Minister Fidel Castro. Some of these unusual plots are covered in Chapter Six.

During the Cold War, the chain of command between president and intelligence agency became such that plausible denial was the name of the game. If there were no clear directives to 'bribe', 'kill' or 'take out' an individual, then it would be harder for their sudden assassination to be linked to the CIA, and more importantly, the president. The dangerous leap between intelligence gathering and assassination was definitely taken by the CIA, marring the world's view of America and its top-secret security agency. While Castro may have escaped, he was not the only high-profile foreign figure to make an appearance on the CIA's 'to do' list, and others weren't so lucky.

Patrice Lumumba (1925-61)

In June 1960, the Democratic Republic of Congo descended into a state of civil war. Previously under Belgian rule, the central African country had recently been declared independent, and some 200 tribes were being ruled by Lumumba, an inexperienced, idealistic politician. With Lumumba not having any real control over the vast country or its mutinying army, the Belgian troops returned to Congo to try and restore order. They were backed by Moise Tshombe, an enemy of Lumumba and a local politician from the wealthy province of Katanga, which wanted to secede from the republic. When Lumumba appealed to the United Nations for troops and support to oust the Belgians, they refused and so he then appealed to the Soviet Union. The CIA already feared Lumumba's pro-communist stance, but they saw the supply of Soviet weapons and technicians as an invitation to communism in central Africa and felt something had to be done.

President Eisenhower called for 'strong action' to be taken against Lumumba and that the only real course of action would be to 'remove' him from the situation. Of course, these words are open to interpretation, but CIA director Allen Dulles believed that Eisenhower had authorised the kill, and a team assembled by the CIA's Africa division was set up. With Lumumba in the custody of the Congolese army, the primary plan involved a poisoned tube of toothpaste, the effects of which would resemble the symptoms of a tropical disease, and there was also a plan involving a sniper. Before either of these could be carried out, Lumumba escaped, and after being tracked down with the help of the CIA, he was handed over to Tshombe's now independent state of Katanga in January 1961. With Tshombe and Belgian officials standing by, Lumumba and two of his colleagues were beaten, dragged into the bush and shot dead. The bodies were later dismembered and dissolved in acid to prevent any trace of them being found.

Ngo Dinh Diem (1901-63)

The ambiguous nature of Eisenhower's words was common during his time, and a similar 'unofficial order' approach could have been applied a few years later, in the case of South Vietnamese president Ngo Dinh Diem, who was killed during a military *coup* on 2 November 1963. The CIA had a strong presence in 1960s Vietnam, and America had supported Diem, believing his popularity would unite the south of the country as a force against the spread of Communism. But Diem's popularity was waning as he attempted to secure the financial future of his own family and establish a stronger Catholic presence in the country, while alienating the Buddhist majority. Many South Vietnamese officers were unhappy with the regime and were prepared to initiate a *coup* if they had American support. While there is little evidence to prove that the Kennedy administration openly offered their backing to the *coup*, many people, including Kennedy's successor, Lyndon B. Johnson, believe that it was his indirect involvement in deaths such as Diem's that led to his own assassination three weeks after the Vietnamese leader's. It is unlikely, however, that General Duong Van Minh would have gone through with the *coup* if he believed that the 16,000-strong US military presence in the country would oppose it. At 1.30 p.m. on 1 November, Diem's presidential palace was attacked, and the prime minister fled, only to be arrested with his brother at a Catholic church the next day. On their way to the military's headquarters, both men were killed en route, and their bodies were buried in unmarked graves. The precise details of their assassination remain unknown.

The ban on assassinations

The good name of the United States had been smeared by the findings of the Church Report. The CIA had hung out its dirty laundry to dry and the American public were in shock. With trust in government and the security services at an all-time low, President Ford issued Executive Order 11905 in 1976, to try and redefine the role of the intelligence services. This order outlawed political assassination, stating, 'No employee of the United States Government shall engage in, or conspire to engage in, political assassination'. The order was upheld by President Carter in 1978, and Reagan in 1981. The ban seemed to lose its clarity in times of war, or in the form of retaliation attacks, as with the bombing of the Bab al-Azizia compound of Libyan leader Muammar Gaddafi in 1986, after he had ordered Libyan agents to bomb a Berlin nightclub frequented by US soldiers. President Bill Clinton also faced this controversial issue in 1998 when Egyptian Islamic Jihadists truck-bombed four of the United States' east African embassies. It has since been revealed that Clinton signed a directive that ordered the capture of Osama bin Laden for his involvement in the attacks. While the primary objective was to bring bin Laden back to the United States to stand trial, the directive also clarified that deadly force could be used if it was deemed impossible to take him alive. This exception of self-defence allowed Clinton's administration to skirt round the ban on assassinations because they believed bin Laden posed an imminent threat to US national security, had previously been involved in attacks on US personnel and was likely to be again. It would be thirteen years before bin Laden was killed by US forces.

Osama bin Laden (1957-2011)

On 1 May 2011, President Barack Obama addressed the American people and told them 'the United States has conducted an operation that killed Osama bin Laden, the leader of Al Qaeda and a terrorist who's responsible for the murder of thousands of innocent men, women and children'. Since the attacks on the World Trade Centre in New York City and the Pentagon on 11 September 2001, Osama bin Laden had become an international hate figure and a symbol of those horrific hijackings. As the head of Al-Qaeda who, in 2004, claimed responsibility for the atrocities, he had managed to remain elusive to the intelligence community for nearly ten years. Obama explained that, not long after becoming president, he instructed the director of the CIA, who at that time was Leon Panetta, to make the capture or killing of bin Laden a top priority in the war against Al Qaeda that was still taking place in Afghanistan. After years of intelligence operations, it emerged in August 2010 that he may have been hiding in a compound in Abbottabad, Pakistan.

At around 1 a.m. Pakistan Standard Time, on 2 May 2011, Operation Neptune Spear was underway. Two Black Hawk helicopters dropped twenty-four elite special force Navy SEALs, a translator and an explosives-sniffing dog outside the compound. Despite Obama saying that 'they took care to avoid civilian casualties', five people, including bin Laden, were killed in the raid. Commandos stormed the main building after shooting bin Laden's personal messenger, Abu Ahmed al-Kuwaiti, and Kuwaiti's brother. Bin Laden's twenty-year-old son, Khalid, and a fourth person were shot dead as the SEALs rushed up the stairs to the top floor of the compound where they believed their primary target was living. Osama bin Laden appeared in a doorway and narrowly escaped fire as he retreated back into the room. His twelve-year-old daughter was wounded by shrapnel and one of his wives was shot in the leg. Following him into the room, the SEALs killed bin Laden with two shots to the chest and one above his left eye. He was not armed, but there were two guns in the room. Identifying the dead man as their target, and reporting back to Panetta, the SEAL force then gathered intelligence materials from the compound and took bin Laden's body with them as they swiftly exited the area by helicopter. The whole operation lasted thirty-eight minutes. The body was then transferred to the USS *Carl Vinson*, a United States Navy supercarrier that was operating in the North Arabian Sea, where DNA analysis was carried out. Islamic rites were performed and bin Laden's body was wrapped in a white shroud and dropped into the ocean to prevent an extremist shrine being created at a gravesite. On the night of bin Laden's assassination, President Obama in the United States said, 'The death of bin Laden marks the most significant achievement to date in our nation's effort to defeat Al-Qaeda… His demise should be welcomed by all who believe in peace and human dignity'.

Means to an end: unusual assassination methods

Death by umbrella

The bizarre death of Bulgarian author and government critic Georgi Markov stands out as one of the most unusual assassination methods in recent history. Markov was a defector who was working for the BBC in London in the 1970s. He had fled Bulgaria in the late 1960s after, rather ironically, writing a play about a military assassination that did not find favour with Bulgarian leader, Todor Zhivkov. He was not silenced, though, and he continued to publish material that criticised the leadership of his homeland. Walking across London's Waterloo Bridge to his night job at the BBC, he suddenly felt a sharp pain in the back of his leg. A man standing in a bus queue, holding an umbrella apologised — he was reported to have had a non-British accent — and then got into a passing taxi. While the incident in itself was not unusual, and Markov continued on his way to work. Later that evening, he felt very ill and went to hospital, believing he had been poisoned. Despite the doctors' best efforts, they were unable to save him and he died a few days later. A post-mortem revealed a tiny pellet containing traces of the highly toxic poison ricin lodged in the skin of Markov's thigh. It is believed the umbrella was used as a device to inject the pellet. While Markov's killer has never been found, he is believed to have been a Bulgarian secret agent, perhaps working with the KGB. In 2008, the case was reopened by Scotland Yard investigators who travelled to Sofia, Bulgaria, to interview witnesses and examine archived documents relating to the unsolved murder.

Although none can quite match up to the methods employed to bring about Markov's end, below are a few more peculiar ways assassins have tried (and failed) to kill their victims.

Rat killer

Stalin's death was officially recorded as natural, but many people in British and American intelligence circles believe that he may have been given a fatal dose of warfarin, an anticoagulant used as a pesticide for rats. Georgy Malenkov and Lavrenti Beria were the last of Stalin's comrades to see him alive when they joined him for dinner on 5 March 1953, the night he suffered a heart attack and died a slow and painful death.

In the news

In 1894, President of the French Republic, Sadi Carnot, was travelling through the city of Lyons in a carriage when Santo Caserio, a baker's apprentice from Milan, came forward holding a newspaper. He had concealed a knife underneath it and immediately dropped the paper and stabbed the president. He shouted, 'Vive l'anarchie!' ('Long live anarchy!') as he killed him.

Fancy a smoke?

In 1954, Soviet intelligence agent Nikolai Khokhlov was assigned to assassinate Georgi Okolovich, a member of the Kremlin-opposed National Alliance of Russian Solidarists (NTS). He was given two electrically operated guns with impressive silencers that contained steel and poisoned bullets. Even more unusually and technologically advanced for the time, the guns were disguised as packets of Chesterfield cigarettes. He did not go through with the killing but turned himself in and defected to the West. Khokhlov would go on to survive an attempt himself in 1957 when, in a revenge attack, Soviet agents slipped radioactive thallium into his coffee at a conference. His skin turned brown and he lost all his hair, but survived.

Magnetic mattress bomb

During World War Two, the same Nikolai Khokhlov who would later turn himself in as an assassin, revealing many of the KGB's secrets and writing a tell-all autobiography, had previously killed Nazi General Kommissar Wilhelm Kube in a planned assassination for the Soviets in 1943. Based in what is now known as Belarus, the SS superior was blown up in his bed at 2 a.m., after Khokhlov had a local woman fix a magnetic bomb to the metal frame of Kube's bed. Khokhlov was able to set the fuse for the TNT cube to explode long after he had escaped.

Camera crew

Afghanistan's Lion of Panjshir, otherwise known as Ahmed Shah Massoud, was the military strategist behind troops who forced the Soviet army to withdraw from Afghanistan in the 1980s. He would then go on to defend the Northern Alliance from the Taliban and Al Qaeda attacks. Probably not coincidentally, two days before 9/11, two Tunisian members of Al Qaeda posing as crew for a Moroccan TV station, arrived where Massoud was living, to conduct what he believed would be a TV interview. They had packed explosives into the camera's battery, which exploded, killing Massoud and both of his assassins. It is likely that Massoud would have been one of America's greatest Afghan allies in their war against the Taliban government and Al Qaeda.

Poison pistol

When Ukrainian exile Stefan Bandera was found dead of a presumed heart attack in Munich in 1959, police noticed tiny cuts on his face caused by fragments of glass and decided to conduct a detailed post-mortem. Their investigation revealed Bandera had died from inhaling a deadly liquid form of cyanide known as prussic acid. Bandera's killer, KGB agent Bogdan Stashynsky, would later defect to the West and describe how the liquid had come from a specially designed weapon that, when fired, crushed a small glass capsule of the poison, releasing it into the atmosphere as a vapour. When inhaled, the poison could kill a person almost immediately.

Oh, Matron!

In 1947, Ukrainian Archbishop Theodore Romzha was recovering in hospital after surviving an attempt on his life — a choreographed vehicle crash sanctioned by the Soviet government, and a subsequent beating had failed to kill him — when a more direct approach was used to finish the job. An agent, posing as a nurse, injected a lethal dose of poison into his veins.

Chapter Five: The Death of a President

The greatest leader of our time has been struck down by the foulest deed of our time
Lyndon B. Johnson

When one considers the assassination rate of the first emperors of Rome and compares it with that of the first men who were sworn in as President of the United States of America, there's no denying the presidents faired extremely well. Despite the fact they were also ruling over the lives of many people and a large, expanding geographical area, the first fifteen presidents, elected by their peers, did not face backstabbing, murderous behaviour from their contemporaries, were not attacked by their bodyguards and definitely weren't slain at the hands of their own family members. It wasn't until seventy-six years after George Washington was first elected that a US president was assassinated, and the country gasped in disbelief that anyone, especially an American citizen, could so easily take the life of their own president. Despite the harsh treatment of all those connected with the conspiracy, future assassins were not deterred and three more presidents would die by similar means, while many more survived daring attempts made on their lives.

While in some countries, a life in politics seems like a stable job with good career prospects, putting yourself forward as the face of new ideas, policies or political parties almost anywhere in the world can be risky business. A successful political life is a very public one, where people feel as if the politician identifies with them because they see them regularly on TV, hear them speak at a rally or even meet them in person. But creating that public image essential for political success is a double-edged sword, especially where the possibility of assassination is concerned. That ease of access and approachability has put many a politician literally in the firing line of dangerous individuals and opposition groups who do not share their views. This has been demonstrated as recently as 2011 when a man tried to kill US Representative Gabrielle Giffords as she met people from her congressional district in a supermarket car park in Tucson, Arizona.

While presidents of the United States have certainly faced more than their fair share of assassination plots, theirs is by no means the only country where the elimination of a politician has occurred in this way. This chapter chronicles the four notorious assassinations of the USA's heads of state, including perhaps the most infamous political killing of all time — that of John F. Kennedy — the various close calls experienced by other more fortunate White House inhabitants and some of the world's most well-known assassinations of those who, for better or worse, chose a life of politics.

Abraham Lincoln (1809-65)

On the day of his assassination in 1865, before heading to the theatre where he would unknowingly meet his end, President Abraham Lincoln remarked to his bodyguard, 'I believe there are men who want to take my life and I have no doubt they will do it. I know no one could do it and escape alive, but if it is to be done, it is impossible to prevent it'. Lincoln's prophesy of how his life would end, and the certainty with which he believed it may, seems startling, but he was aware of his many enemies and how his political decisions and the tension of civil war put his life at risk. Of course, he couldn't have known how easily, and how soon after he spoke these words, his life would be taken.

Victim

For one of the most famous presidents in US history, Abraham Lincoln came from a relatively poor and simple background. Raised as the son of a Kentucky farmer, with about a year's formal education to his name, Lincoln's rise to political power is an extraordinary feat in itself. It was his 'everyman' background, warm nature and intelligence beyond his station, and childhood circumstance that made him so likeable and relatable to many Americans. And so it was that, on 6 November 1860, this self-taught lawyer from Illinois, who had spent just two years serving as a member of the House of Representatives and had never held a position as state governor or mayor, was elected as the next president of the United States, with 40 per cent of the vote. Despite not holding a position of public office for ten years prior to his victory, Lincoln had become a powerful public speaker whose honesty, integrity and uncompromising belief in his own principles, made him a winning candidate. It also helped him that the Democratic Party was unable to decide where it stood on the issue of slavery, and put forward two opposing candidates for the ballot, thus allowing Lincoln to take the lead. Indeed, it was Lincoln's own views on slavery (see below) that indirectly led to his death, just four years after he was inaugurated.

Assassination

In a scene suitably dramatic for the setting, Lincoln was shot at point-blank range in the back of the head while attending a performance of *Our American Cousin* at Ford's Theatre in Washington. It was no secret that Lincoln would be attending the play on 14 April 1865, just five days after Confederate General Robert E. Lee had surrendered to Ulysses S. Grant at Appomattox. Despite the increased risk to his life at that time, Lincoln refused to cancel his plans and arrived as expected at the fashionable venue. Lincoln was joined in the state box by his wife Mary Todd Lincoln, Senator Ira Harris's daughter, Clara, and her fiancé Major Henry Rathbone. General Grant was supposed to join Lincoln with his own wife for the event, but pulled out at the last minute. At 10 o'clock, Lincoln's assassin, John Wilkes Booth, who had been drinking whiskey at the bar next door, arrived at the theatre, purchased tobacco from the ticket seller and made his way to Lincoln's box. The sole police officer whose duty it was to protect Lincoln had left his post at the door to visit a nearby pub, and the only person between Booth and Lincoln was a White House coachman, who let Booth, a well-known theatrical actor, into the box without question. Booth waited for a crude line in the play, which elicited a loud laugh from the audience and then fired his .44 Derringer pistol into the back of Lincoln's head behind his left ear. Henry Rathbone lunged at Booth who quickly dropped his gun and drew a knife, slashing the major's arm. Booth then leapt off the box's railing and onto the stage, but one of the spurs from his boots got caught in a flag draped from the railing and he fell awkwardly, breaking his left shinbone. He hobbled off the stage while the audience looked on, horrified, and out through a door into an alleyway where a horse was waiting for him. The first man to kill an American president then rode off into the night. Lincoln would die ten hours later in a house opposite the theatre, with his devastated wife by his side.

Assassin

It's fitting that John Wilkes Booth chose a theatre as the setting for his murderous act. Booth came from a theatrical family and had worked as an actor playing leading roles in a number of Shakespeare plays. His father, Junius Brutus Booth, named after Marcus Brutus, one of Julius Caesar's assassins, was one of the most well-known actors in America during the first half of the nineteenth century. Booth had strong views about the civil war and slavery. He supported the South and the Confederate cause, and he became a member of the Virginia militia. While he was not directly involved in the civil war, he decided to do his part by plotting with others to kidnap the president. He had planned to kidnap Lincoln from Ford's Theatre in January that year, and again while he was out riding in March, but both plots failed to materialise, and then Booth turned his attention to the April assassination.

Lincoln's death was, in fact, part of a bigger plot to bring about the downfall of the Union. Booth's co-conspirators, George Atzerodt and Lewis Powell (tried as Lewis Paine), were intending to kill Vice President Andrew Johnson and Secretary of State William H. Seward respectively. On the night Booth shot Lincoln at 10 p.m., Powell broke into Seward's house and attacked him with a knife. He badly injured Seward's face and neck, but did not manage to kill him. Atzerodt, meanwhile, backed out of the plan at the last minute and decided to get drunk instead. Booth was also aided by David Herold, with whom he met up after leaving the theatre.

Motives

Abraham Lincoln believed in the strength of the Union and was determined not to see it fall apart. In one sense, slavery was a side issue to his cause — he once said, if he could save the Union without freeing any slave, he would do it. Lincoln had repeatedly said that, once elected president, he would not try and change the Southern states' existing slavery laws, but he made it quite clear that he opposed the extension of slavery to other new territories that might join the Union, believing that, if he could stop the growth of slavery, it would soon die out in the South. The civil war erupted after some of the Southern states decided to leave the Union precisely for this reason, resulting in eleven states in total identifying thcmselves as Confederate. When the Confederate army besieged military garrison Fort Sumter in South Carolina and opened fire on 13 April 1861, the civil war began. Lincoln's views on slavery seemed to change as the war progressed. He realised the unharnessed military power of the Southern slaves who had fled to the North and, as an act of war, delivered the 'Proclamation of Emancipation' on 22 September 1862, freeing all slaves. As supporters of the Confederate cause, the conspirators were caught up in the drama and emotions of wartime. Kidnapping or even assassinating the leading figure of the Union would have seemed to them the ultimate bargaining tool or game-changer in the war. Booth attended a speech Lincoln made at a White House celebration on 11 April, in which he supported freedom, education and voting rights for former black slaves. Disgusted by the thought of former slaves becoming akin to United States citizens, Booth vowed this would be the last speech Lincoln would make. It was, in fact, his final public address. This speech, combined with Confederate General Robert E. Lee's surrender, just days before the planned date for Lincoln's assassination, was perhaps the final encouragement Booth and company needed to put their plan into action. Despite some conspiracies surrounding the Confederacy's involvement in Lincoln's assassination, it became clear from Booth's diary, after the fact that the scheme was devised without the aid of a puppet master, and his actions were a result of his own feelings of hatred for Lincoln and the policies Lincoln stood for.

Aftermath

Lincoln was right when he prophesied that anyone who killed him wouldn't escape alive, although his assassin wasn't going down without a fight. Not only did Booth make it out of the theatre and across the Potomac River to the home of Dr Samuel Mudd, a Confederacy sympathiser, who set his injured leg, he travelled with Herold across the Rappahannock River into Virginia to a farm near Port Royal. Witnesses had identified Booth at the scene, and Secretary of War, Edwin M. Stanton, had ordered his arrest with a combined $100,000 reward on the heads of three of the wanted conspirators: Booth, Herold and John Surratt, who had been involved in the failed plot to kill Lincoln, but were believed to be part of the April assassination as well. Police tracked Booth and Herold to a tobacco barn on a farm nearly two weeks after the assassination. They ordered the two men to come out and surrender — Herold did, but Booth remained inside, so the police set the building on fire. Booth was dragged from the burning barn and appeared to be shot. Although it's possible a police officer shot the assassin, others believe Booth shot himself. He died a few hours later on 26 April 1865. With Booth dead, eight other conspirators were named by the government, captured and brought to trial in May and June 1865. The trial has since been heavily criticised: witnesses were intimidated by the prosecution and key evidence was withheld, including the diaries of Confederate President Jefferson Davis and Booth himself. The eight conspirators were found guilty on 6 July and sentenced. One received a six-year prison sentence, three other conspirators were given life sentences (and were later pardoned in 1869), while four people, Herold, Paine, Atzerodt and John Surratt's mother, Mary, were hung for their involvement in the assassination plots. Jefferson Davis was charged with conspiring with the plotters and, despite never being brought to trial, served two years in prison.

Booth was pro-slavery and pro-secession, and believed that the death of Lincoln would bring about the end of slavery abolitionism and the northern President Abraham Lincoln states ruling over the South. He was wrong. President Andrew Johnson, who succeeded Lincoln, initially aimed to keep the restoration of the Union on the political agenda, but Congress, without the leadership of Lincoln, pushed for the abolition of slavery and the disenfranchisement of many ex-Confederates. Lincoln's death was just as hurtful to the South as it was to his supporters — it took longer to achieve reconciliation without him, and slavery was no more. Lincoln still remains one of America's most popular and revered presidents.

Who really *killed Lincoln?*

There was little doubt that Lincoln's death, the attack on William H. Seward and the planned attack on Andrew Johnson, which occurred at the same time, were part of a conspiracy involving a number of individuals who had failed to kidnap Lincoln for the Confederacy and then decided to kill him instead. But in the highly-charged aftermath of Lincoln's death, a number of conspiracy theories emerged over who was really behind the death of the president.

— **Confederate leaders:** Confederate President Jefferson Davis was captured on 10 May 1865 and kept prisoner for two years. Although there was virtually no evidence to suggest Davis had any knowledge of the plot, let alone ordered it, the political climate at the time meant that there was good reason for Davis to have been involved — Lincoln had ordered a raid on Richmond, Virginia, where Davis was residing, with the hopes of capturing or killing Davis himself. Booth had connections with the Confederate Secret Service and had informed them of his plan to kidnap Lincoln. It's possible one of Davis's subordinates suggested an assassination might be more effective.

— **The vice president:** Initially, the man who politically benefited the most from Lincoln's death was his second-in-command, Andrew Johnson, a senator from Tennessee, who was the only Southern senator in favour of the Union, and who was famous for getting drunk at Lincoln's inauguration. The year after Lincoln's death, Congress set up a committee to investigate Johnson's possible involvement. The only evidence linking him to Booth a mysterious card left at the hotel where Johnson was staying on the night of Lincoln's death. It said, 'Don't wish to disturb you. Are you at home? J. Wilkes Booth'. Johnson struggled to gain much support from Congress during his presidency, was the first president to face impeachment and left office after only three years, in 1869.

— **The Secretary of War:** Another popular name put forward as the man behind Booth's plan was that of Edwin Stanton, Lincoln's Secretary of War. It was well known that Stanton opposed Lincoln's plan for reconstruction of the Southern states and wanted to see more military occupation there after the war. But largely, the evidence against him has been widely refuted: he refused to allow Major Eckert, his assistant, to attend the theatre with Lincoln as a bodyguard (but perhaps he was trying to put Lincoln off from going, as he knew it was dangerous for the president to make public appearances so soon after Lee's surrender). He allegedly allowed Booth to make a getaway as he failed to send a telegram ordering guards to arrest Booth on his way to Maryland, only to cover his tracks by having him killed, and he ripped out eighteen pages from Booth's diary, which was reportedly intact when it was handed into his care. Of course, the arguments that Stanton was unable to send a telegram to that part of Maryland and that the pages had been ripped out by Booth himself, who used his diary as a notepad, both hold water.

— **The other Booth:** There were even suggestions that the man killed at the Virginia farmhouse was not Booth at all, but a man named J. W. Boyd, the real killer, who had been hired to carry out the attack on Booth's behalf. Some claimed to have seen Booth after his reported death and said he was living under a new name. Even though the dead body at the farmhouse was identified as Booth, with some trouble by the family doctor and family members, his body was not released to the family until 1869. One man in Oklahoma even claimed on his deathbed to be Booth. His body was mummified by a mortician and displayed at sideshows as an attraction for many years afterwards.

Mary Surratt

On 7 July 1865, four people were hanged for their part in the Lincoln assassination. One of those was Mary Surratt, the mother of John Surratt, who went into hiding immediately after the assassination. He was finally captured and extradited to the US from Egypt and was put on trial for his involvement in the assassination plot but was eventually released after a mistrial. John had been involved in the original Lincoln kidnap plot after Dr Samuel Mudd had introduced him to John Wilkes Booth. Mrs Surratt ran a boarding house where her son John lived, and where other conspirators stayed. Some believe the plot to assassinate Lincoln was planned there. She was arrested after police who came to her house to question her were shocked when Lewis Powell, the man who had attempted to kill Seward, showed up coincidentally. Despite Surratt's protests that she did not know Powell, she was arrested and placed in a makeshift cell on board a prison ship. There was no firm evidence to suggest Mrs Surratt knew what the men had planned, and much of the testimony in court against her has since been proved false or was shown to be obtained from witnesses under duress. On the day of the hanging, it was believed President Andrew Johnson would pardon Surratt because of her age and her sex, and soldiers were placed on every block between the White House and the execution site to quickly transmit the pardon message. But no pardon came, and she became the first US woman to be hanged under federal law. Many historians believe Surratt was put on trial and sentenced to hang to entice her son to come forward and take her place, but he never did.

The Kennedy connection

Two of the most famous assassinations in American history are undoubtedly those of presidents Abraham Lincoln and John F. Kennedy. Unusually, and to the delight of conspiracy theorists, there is a number of bizarre coincidences between the two deaths. Here are just a few interesting connections between the lives and deaths of both men:

— **100 years:** Lincoln was elected president in 1860. Exactly 100 years later, Kennedy was elected. Lincoln's assassin, John Wilkes Booth is believed to have been born in 1839, while Lee Harvey Oswald, who shot Kennedy, was born in 1939. The two men who took over from these assassinated presidents were born 100 years apart.

— **Where? When? Why?:** Lincoln was shot in the head in Ford's Theatre, while Kennedy was shot in the head in a Lincoln car made by Ford. They were both shot on a Friday, in the company of their wives. They both supported greater racial equality and were shot by Southern men with extreme views.

— **Johnson:** Both presidents' successors shared the last name Johnson. Andrew Johnson and Lyndon B. Johnson both have thirteen letters in their names.

— **Killers:** Both killers were shot before they faced trial. Booth carried out his assassination in a theatre, while Oswald was finally apprehended in a movie theatre. The full names of both killers contain fifteen letters.

Lucky escape: Andrew Jackson (1767-1845)

Thirty years before John Wilkes Booth held the gun to Lincoln's head and pulled the trigger, President Andrew Jackson became the first US President to face an assassination attempt. On 13 January 1835, after attending the funeral of a congressman, Jackson was walking through the Capitol building's rotunda in Washington DC, when a man drew out a percussion cap gun and fired at him from about three metres away. The gun's ignition cap exploded, making a sound, but the bullet did not leave the barrel. Jackson, shocked by the sound, launched on the gunman and beat him with his cane. The assassin had a second loaded gun in his pocket, and fired that, but the same problem occurred and Jackson remained unharmed. The unsuccessful assassin was a housepainter called Richard Lawrence, who displayed unusual behaviour and believed he was the rightful heir to the British throne. A jury found him not responsible for his actions at the time of the shooting due to his mental state, and he spent the rest of his life in mental institutions. Andrew Jackson believed Lawrence had been hired by his political enemies, although they denied any involvement and accused him of using the event to garner sympathy from the American people.

Spencer Perceval (1762-1812)

Victim

Many men (and one woman) have led the government of Great Britain since the 1700s, but in all that time, and through all the changes in power and policies, only one British prime minister has ever been assassinated. That sad honour goes to Spencer Perceval, a barrister who fathered thirteen children and became First Lord of the Treasury (the prime minister of his time) in 1809. He was a member of the Tory party, whose weak parliament's casual approach to economics saw many of Britain's working-class face poverty. When he was shot, three years into his time in office, many thought a workers' revolutionary group was behind his death. During Perceval's term, skilled textile artisans saw their jobs disappearing when new mechanised looms were introduced, and a violent uprising ensued. Perceval's assassin was not a textile worker, however, but a mentally unstable man who held a personal grudge towards the government.

Assassination

On Monday, 11 May 1812, a man described as a tall, sombre figure wearing a 'snuff-coloured suit', waited in the lobby of the House of Commons, keeping watch for the prime minister. Not long after Perceval arrived — he was in a rush coming from Downing Street and walked briskly through the lobby to the entrance to the Commons — the sombre figure blocked his path, raised an arm and fired point-blank into Perceval's chest. Onlookers saw a curling wreath of smoke rise above the prime minister's head and then watched as he staggered and fell to the floor, a small trickle of blood falling from his lips.

The man had shot Perceval in the heart with a large bullet, killing him almost instantly, but the assassin made no attempt to escape, and when one of the Commons officers cried out, 'Where is the rascal that fired?', he stepped forward and gave himself up. An MP for Liverpool named General Gascoigne grabbed hold of the assailant with such force that he almost broke the man's arm, and another loaded pistol was found concealed in his pocket.

Assassin

General Gascoigne recognised Perceval's killer, largely because he was known in the Houses of Parliament since February that year when he started hassling MPs to support a compensation claim. His name was John Bellingham. Originally from Huntingdonshire, the thirty-five-year-old had lived a rather unfortunate life. His father had spent some time in a mental asylum and died insane, he was involved in a shipwreck while working for the East India Service, had previously lost his house in a fire and had been declared bankrupt. After finding work as a commission agent for a Liverpool-based merchant's office, he was sent to Russia, where he became involved in a dispute over a debt he owed and found himself imprisoned for five years there. On his return to England, he blamed the government for his misfortune and, after a compensation claim was ignored by the prime minister, he began pestering other MPs for their support. It was in April 1812 that he bought two guns and ammunition, and had a deep pocket made inside his coat in preparation for his attack on Perceval.

Aftermath

No real attempt was made by Bellingham to escape — he was identified at the scene of the crime and detained briefly in the prison room of the sergeant-at-arms before being relocated to Newgate Prison. He appeared in court at the Old Bailey less than a week later on 15 May, where a plea of insanity was refused. The judge refused to allow Bellingham, who defended himself, to present witnesses giving evidence of his mental state — he made it clear he had intended to kill Perceval because he was ruined by the prime minister's refusal to see that justice was done and compensation was paid to him. There was no real precedent in Great Britain for assessing an assassin's mental state, so it took the jury just ten minutes to find him guilty of murder. He was hanged three days later at Newgate Prison.

James Garfield (1831-81)

James Garfield's assassin did not conspire with others to bring about the end of America's leading political figure. He did not have an escape route or a clear political motive for his actions, but instead killed the president in a planned attack of psychotic revenge. He believed the president should pay for his ingratitude and took the steps to see that it was done. This assassination may not have been trying to change the course of history but is illustrative of the earlier threat to high-profile figures, the ease with which a lone gunman, even in the 1800s, could wipe out an important politician, and how even an insane man could act determinedly and rationally in planning and executing an assassination.

Victim

James A. Garfield was the twentieth president of the United States and had previously served as a member of Congress for Ohio for nine consecutive terms. Because of his assassination, his presidency lasted just 200 days, the second-shortest in US history. Garfield came from a humble farming background, and it was through ambition and determination that he entered the political arena after graduating from college, aged twenty-six. He served as a Major General for the Unionists during the civil war, was considered a skilled public speaker and was elected to the US senate in 1880, the same year he was nominated for president and narrowly won the election. While he may not have swept the board with the American vote, the people would never get to see what kind of president he would become. He was struck down two months shy of his fiftieth birthday.

Assassination

On 2 July 1881, Garfield, together with his secretary of state, James G. Blaine, and others, were making their way through the passenger terminal of Baltimore and Potomac Railroad Station on Missouri Avenue in Washington DC. The president was due to catch a train north to Massachusetts and Williams College for his college reunion, where he was to deliver a speech. Suddenly, Charles Julius Guiteau, appeared and fired two shots from a .44 calibre Bulldog pistol. One shot nicked the president's arm, while the other entered his back and lodged somewhere inside his body. Guiteau was immediately seized by security guards and arrested. The president was rushed to the White House to receive medical treatment.

Assassin

Guiteau was born in 1841 and was from Freeport, Illinois. Despite qualifying as a lawyer in Chicago in 1869, Guiteau, who had a rather unstable upbringing, spent much of his life being out of work and committing petty fraud to make ends meet. He had a dalliance with a New York religious group in his twenties that preached free love and communal living. Then, after a divorce from his librarian wife in 1874, he began to lose his grip on reality, living off next to nothing and acting as a religious preacher, and then as a self-proclaimed campaigner for the Republican Party. It was his campaigning for Garfield in the 1880 presidential election that cemented the president's fate.

Motives

Guiteau believed that a speech he had written in favour of Garfield, and had printed and distributed, was largely responsible for the president narrowly winning the election —

it is disputed as to whether Garfield ever delivered this speech. In his muddled mind, Guiteau felt that Garfield owed him a debt of gratitude for his campaigning. He had sent letters to the president and his secretary of state requesting a position as a foreign diplomat in Vienna and Paris, believing he would 'represent the United States government ... with dignity and grace'. He also suggested that he should be married to the daughter of a deceased New York Republican millionaire. Given Guiteau's status, station and situation, it's very unlikely that Garfield and his aides would have given much thought to these rather bizarre letters as they tried to get their new government in order. Guiteau also made himself known to the White House staff by requesting information about his career prospects. When nothing materialised, Guiteau felt betrayed by the president he had supported, and vowed to take the president's life.

Aftermath

Arguably, Guiteau did not succeed in killing James Garfield. Of course, the bullet that he fired brought about the end of Garfield's life, but had modern medicine, or even basic hygiene standards, been applied by the doctors who treated him, it's possible Garfield could have gone on to serve the rest of his presidential term. At least sixteen doctors were brought in to try and locate the bullet, which is believed to have lodged in Garfield's spine or his lung. Today's practice of washing hands and sterilising medical equipment was not commonly used by doctors at the time, and the careless poking and prodding of Garfield's wounds led to bacterial infections, which were compounded by further operations to try and remove infected matter. Scientist and inventor Alexander Graham Bell was brought in to see if a device that resembled a primitive metal detector could locate the bullet. With no success in this, Garfield was relocated to a house by the sea in New Jersey, where he died on 19 September, two and a half months after the shooting.

When Guiteau was brought to trial two months after Garfield's death, his defence tried to argue that it was medical malpractice that had ended Garfield's life, rather than Guiteau. He also tried to enter an insanity plea; both arguments were turned down by the court. Despite Guiteau's clear mental instability, he was tried as a sane man and was found guilty after just one hour of jury deliberation. He was sentenced to death by hanging, which was carried out in front of a large crowd of spectators at the District of Columbia Prison on 30 June 1882.

William McKinley (1843-1901)

Victim

Born on 29 January 1843, in Niles, Ohio, McKinley was just fifty-eight when his life was brought to an abrupt end. McKinley had been a Union soldier during the civil war and was elected to Congress in 1876. He later served as Governor of Ohio before being elected as president in 1896. McKinley guided victorious US forces into the ten-week Spanish-American war of 1898, and was elected for a second term in 1900, a year before he was assassinated.

Assassination

On 6 September 1901, President William McKinley was in Buffalo, New York, to attend the Pan American Exposition. He had delivered a speech the previous day, praising the importance of the event, and was visiting the exposition's auditorium and concert hall, known as the Temple of Music, at 4 p.m. that day. He was shaking hands with visitors to the exposition when he suddenly faced Leon Czolgosz in the chaotic line up. Czolgosz had a handkerchief wrapped around his right hand, which may have appeared to McKinley to be a bandage. Before the president could offer his other hand to shake, two shots were fired from a .32 calibre, short-barrelled revolver concealed beneath the handkerchief. Similar to James Garfield's injuries, one bullet caused just a flesh wound, while the other was more severe, burying itself in McKinley's stomach. The crowd in the busy auditorium descended on Czolgosz, who was pushed to the ground, and started beating him up, before rioting broke out as news of the attack spread and soldiers were deployed to keep the peace.

Assassin

Leon Czolgosz was a Polish-American who had been raised on a farm near Cleveland. He had worked in factories since the age of sixteen, and he was twenty-eight when he decided to assassinate McKinley. Czolgosz's adult life had seen him veer towards the anarchist movement — he became obsessed with anarchists and the widely reported behaviour of men such as Gaetano Bresci, who travelled from the US to Italy to kill King Umberto I. In 1898, he seemed to have suffered some kind of mental shift and quit his job, returned to his family's farm and focused his attentions on reading about anarchist movements and brutal authoritarian rule. When Czolgosz moved to Chicago and tried to become part of the anarchist underground groups there, he was not made welcome. His bizarre behaviour and desperation meant he was labelled as a 'loose cannon' and treated as such. Anarchists went so far as to refer to him in an anarchist publication as a possible police spy. Facing rejection from a group of people who supposedly went against the grain was probably a lot for the unbalanced Czolgosz to handle, and perhaps his later act of killing McKinley was done in part to prove something to those anarchists who had doubted he was one of them.

Motives

Undoubtedly Czolgosz's readings and anarchist education influenced his decision to assassinate the president. It's possible that he looked up to anarchists such as the Russian People's Will, Bresci and Santo Caerio who killed the president of France in 1894 and saw the chance to free US citizens from an oppressive regime through the removal of their leader. It's also likely that Czolgosz was seeking acceptance from the anarchist groups he longed to be a part of and relished the notoriety that would be associated with such a high-profile act. On the day of Czolgosz's execution, he shouted, 'I did it for the help of the good people, the working men of all countries!' Whatever the activists of Chicago thought of him in life, in the face of death, he was a true anarchist.

Aftermath

In a scene eerily similar to the one that followed the Garfield shooting, McKinley's fate lay in the hands of the doctors who administered to him. Unfortunately, the emergency treatment room at the exposition was poorly equipped, and the surgeon on site was fairly inexperienced. He was unable to locate the bullet that had lodged in McKinley's stomach and sewed up the wound with the bullet still inside. One of the first X-ray machines was on display at the exhibition, but it was not used to detect the bullet, perhaps because the effects of X-rays were not widely understood and those present were afraid of the impact the machine might have on the president. The wound soon became infected and McKinley died eight days later, on 14 September.

Just nine days after McKinley passed away, Czolgosz's trial began. His insanity plea was rejected, and he was found guilty and sentenced to death. The electric chair had been introduced as a more humane form of execution than hanging about ten years previously, making Czolgosz one of the first high-profile victims to face death by electrocution in the US.

Lucky escape: Theodore Roosevelt (1858-1919)

On 14 October 1912, President Theodore Roosevelt was visiting Milwaukee, Wisconsin as part of his campaign for his third presidential term elections. He was not the only non-Wisconsin native to be visiting the city that day. A New York bartender named John Schrank had followed the president on the trail and finally caught up with him. According to his later testimony, he had had dreams in which assassinated former President William McKinley had appeared to him and pointed an accusatory finger at Roosevelt. He believed he had to avenge McKinley's death by assassinating the current president. Roosevelt was on his way to the Milwaukee Auditorium to deliver a speech when he climbed into an open-top car and was shot in the chest by Schrank, who was brandishing a .38 revolver. The bullet penetrated Roosevelt's metal spectacle case and his speech notes before entering his chest. Schrank was wrestled to the ground by policemen as he tried to fire a second shot. He was later declared insane and committed to a mental institution where he died. Schrank may not have achieved what he set out to do that day, but Roosevelt certainly did. Rather than be rushed to hospital, he insisted on delivering his speech while he lost blood from the wound. His opening lines were, 'I don't know whether you fully understand I have just been shot; but it takes more than a bear to kill a bull moose'. When Roosevelt died from a blood clot seven years later, he still had the bullet lodged in his chest.

Lucky escape: Franklin D. Roosevelt (1882-1945)

Less than three weeks before his presidential inauguration on 15 February 1933, Franklin D. Roosevelt learnt first-hand the daily risk that comes with being the president of the United States. Roosevelt had been enjoying a yachting vacation in Florida, preparing for the pressures and challenges that lay ahead, but had decided to stop off in Miami's Bayside Park to make a speech to a small gathering of people. Also in Miami was Chicago Mayor Anton Cermak, who was staying away from his city to avoid trouble from the Chicago mafia, whose boss, Frank Nitti, had recently been wounded by Chicago police. After Roosevelt had made his speech from the backseat of his open-top car, a man carrying a .38 pistol and standing on a chair about seven metres away, showered the area where the president-elect was with gunfire. Five people were hit in the attack, one of whom was Cermak, but Roosevelt remained unharmed. Cermak, who died in hospital three weeks after the shooting, wrongly believed that he was the target of the assassination.

The assassin was an Italian-born bricklayer from New Jersey called Giuseppe Zangara, who was anti-capitalist and against society in general. He fantasised about killing heads of state and politicians, and later said he would have tried to kill any other prominent politician instead, had they been there. He had previously plotted to kill King Victor Emmanuel III in his native Italy and dreamed of killing the previous president, Herbert Hoover. Initially, Zangara was sentenced to eighty years in prison for the shootings, but after Cermak's death, he was sentenced to death for murder and faced his own end on the electric chair on 20 March, just over a month after the shootings took place.

Huey Long (1893-1935)

Victim

Senator Huey P. Long was not the president of the United States but if you'd been in Louisiana in 1935, you might have mistaken him for such. As somewhat of a Robin Hood figure, despite running his state similarly to a dictator, Long had brought more wealth and prosperity to the working classes of Louisiana than his predecessors. With his 'take from the rich, give to the poor' attitude, he had increased taxes for large corporations and used the money to improve education, and to set up an impressive road-building programme in the state. He had also established a wealth distribution movement and spoken openly in the senate about the obligation for rich Americans to support the needs of the poor. Of course, you can't please all the people all of the time, and Long's policies had brought him a number of enemies, many of whom would have been outraged by his plan to run for president, which he announced in August 1935, a month before he was assassinated.

Assassination

On Sunday evening, 8 September 1935 in Baton Rouge, Louisiana, Senator Long was attending a meeting of the Louisiana Legislature at the newly constructed State Capitol Building, discussing a number of issues, including a plan to oust his opponent Judge Benjamin Pavy from his job. At 9.20 p.m., he left the office, and, surrounded by an entourage of armed guards, walked out into the corridor. According to the most widely believed version of events, it was then that a man named Dr Carl Weiss approached the senator, drew a Belgian

.32 automatic pistol and fired a shot into his abdomen. Long's bodyguards retaliated, shooting approximately sixty rounds and killing the assassin. Long, however, was not dead — he stumbled down the steps of the Capitol building and rallied an associate to take him to the hospital. Once there, an operation was performed to repair the damage done by the bullet, but the doctors failed to notice a perforation of his kidney, and on the morning of 10 September, he died from internal bleeding.

Assassin

There was no official investigation into Long's assassination, but the man who approached the senator at the Capitol Building that day was a Louisiana physician named Carl Weiss. At only twenty-nine, he was widely respected in the community and was the son-in-law of Judge Benjamin Pavy. When he left his wife at home on the evening of 8 September, he told her he was going to make house calls on patients and gave no indication that he was planning to kill the senator.

Motive

Many people doubted that Weiss had intended to kill Senator Long, but that doesn't mean he didn't have motive. His father-in-law had strongly opposed Long's policies and openly criticised him in his parish. The senator had retaliated by attacking the Pavy family, seeing to it that two of his daughters lost their teaching jobs, and making accusations that the judge's wife was the illegitimate daughter of her father's black mistress. This would have been very distressing for Weiss's wife and his father-in-law, but was it enough for him to want to risk his own life and kill the senator? Some believed that Weiss had only intended to punch Long in the face and that the bodyguards overreacted by opening fire. With no autopsy performed on Long's body, and Weiss having been killed at the scene, no alternative explanation for what happened that day has emerged.

Aftermath

Unfortunately for the poorer people of Louisiana, many of Long's policies died with him that day. After his death, a period of corruption followed where those who had promised to enforce the senator's 'share the wealth' programme, kept the money for themselves and killed the dream Long had mapped out for the state. The dictatorial style of Long had succeeded in keeping the more deviant Louisiana officials in line, but with him gone, there was no one slapping the wrists of the corrupt and greedy politicians and law makers, who quickly descended into an embarrassing period of indictments and prosecutions for their wrongdoings. But Long was popular in death as much as in life, with some 200,000 mourners turning out for his funeral. His name was the start of a dynasty that saw twelve members of his family join the political sphere.

Failed assassins

Names: Oscar Collazo and Griselio Torresola.

Profiles: Collazo, 36, and Torresola, 25, were two Puerto Rican men from New York. Both were members of the Puerto Rican Nationalist Party which wanted independence for Puerto Rico from the United States. Collazo was a family man who hated the way Puerto Ricans were being discriminated against in New York, and Torresola came from a nationalist family and had experience in using guns.

Target: President Harry S. Truman.

Motive: Collazo and Torresola probably believed the death of the American president at the hands of two Puerto Ricans would have helped their cause, encouraging more of their countrymen to rise up against American rule.

Time of attack: 2.20 p.m., 1 November 1950.

Location: Blair House, Pennsylvania Avenue, Washington DC. Blair House was the temporary residence of the president, as the White House was undergoing renovations.

Plan of action: Unlike other assassins who carefully plotted their assassination attempts, Collazo and Torresola didn't have much of a plan at all. They arrived in Washington only the day prior to their attempt, and briefly scoped out the building they believed the president would be in. The two men did not know for sure that Truman would be in the building at the time of their attack, it just so happened that he was inside taking a nap. The front of the building had three entrances, two basement entrances and one at the top of a flight of steps, and was protected by five guards. The assassins had concealed handguns and ammunition and decided to approach the building from opposite ends to see if they could shoot their way in past the guards.

What happened next: The failed assassination attempt of Harry S. Truman lasted around three minutes. In that time, Collazo approached the main entrance and tried to shoot Private Donald Birdzell who was on guard duty, but when he pulled the trigger, nothing happened. After banging his fist against the gun, he managed to hit Birdzell in the leg, but then quickly came under fire from two guards to the east of the building and Birdzell, who was injured on the ground. Collazo was soon shot in the chest by a Secret Service agent. Torresola, meanwhile, had approached the west basement door and shot Private Leslie Coffelt three times at point-blank range, as well as Private Joseph Downs. The entrance to the building was clear, but before he could get inside, he was shot in the head by

Coffelt, who himself was mortally wounded. Torresola fell down dead.

Aftermath: Collazo survived his chest wound and was later sentenced to death for his actions. His sentence was reduced to life imprisonment by Truman, and then in 1979, he was released by Jimmy Carter. He lived out the rest of his years in Puerto Rico.

John F. Kennedy (1917-63)

Victim

Born in Brookline, Massachusetts on 29 May 1917, John Fitzgerald Kennedy would grow up to become the 35th President of the United States, famous in life, but more famous in death for his appalling assassination and the shockwaves it sent through the American people, and around the world. Kennedy had been a Navy torpedo boat commander during the 1940s and had entered the world of politics when he was elected to Congress as a Democratic Representative from Massachusetts in 1946. Six years later, he became a senator and made his bid for the White House in 1960, when he beat Richard Nixon in a close vote, becoming, at the age of forty-three, the youngest person elected to the office of president. Kennedy spent two months short of three years as president, and in that time, oversaw the Cuban Missile Crisis, key years of the African-American Civil Rights Movements and even declared America's commitment to walking on the moon in the Space Race. Dallas, Texas, was known for its right-wing extremism, and there was some trepidation when Kennedy visited there in 1963, a year before the next presidential election, to try and win over some voters. He brought his wife Jacqueline along for support — it was hoped her glamour would help to negate any bad feeling towards his office.

Assassination

The Kennedy assassination is one few people do not have a mental image of, in large part because of Abraham Zapruder's 8mm camera footage that captured the event in all its gore: the black Lincoln Continental state car driving slowly through downtown Dallas when suddenly a shot fires out, hitting Kennedy in the head; and the final image of Jacqueline Kennedy, in that charming pink suit, sprawling over the back of the open-top car towards a Secret Service agent.

That fateful day of 22 November 1963 began as planned — Kennedy, his wife and aides touched down in Love Field airport, Dallas at 11.25 a.m. The motorcade left thirty minutes later and headed for central Dallas. Six people were in the state car: upfront was the driver Bill Greer and Secret Service bodyguard Roy Kellerman, in the middle row sat Texas Governor John Connally with his wife Nellie, and behind them, the Kennedys.

There had been some initial concern about the crowds responding with hostility towards Kennedy, but those were put to rest when the motorcade travelled down Main Street and was greeted with cheers and waves. The crowd thinned out a bit as the cars and motorcycles drove through Dealey Plaza, passing the Old Courthouse and County Criminal Courts on Houston Street, but there were still a number of people lining the road and waving from the grassy verges when the convoy made a sharp turn onto Elm Street and slowed to 11.2 mph. At 12.30 p.m., as the black Lincoln made its way about halfway down Elm Street, the shots were fired. Many people believed fireworks had been set off, or that it was a car backfiring. The president appeared to grab his chest, which some in the crowd saw as a comedic reaction to the noise. Seconds later, there was no doubt in anyone's mind that someone had just tried to kill the President.

Despite in-depth analysis of the photos, video footage and eyewitness reports, it is still debated as to how many shots were fired, and whether they came from more than one direction. What is known is that Kennedy was hit twice, once in the side of the neck also injuring his back and a second shot that blew off the side of his skull. Governor Connally was also injured in the back and wrist. Once she realised her husband had been shot, Jacqueline scrambled over the back of the car, while a Secret Service agent jumped onto the car towards her as she shouted, 'They've killed Jack; they've killed my husband'. The car then sped off to Parkland Hospital where Kennedy was pronounced dead at 1 p.m.

Assassin

The man charged, but never convicted, with the assassination of President Kennedy was Lee Harvey Oswald. Oswald was a former US Marine who had defected to the Soviet Union in 1959. He returned to the US in 1962, with a Russian wife, after growing bored with life in Moscow, but his reappearance after defecting did not raise any questions. While living in New Orleans, he openly campaigned in favour of Fidel Castro's right to rule Cuba and visited the Soviet and Cuban embassies in Mexico the same year Kennedy was killed, which led to much speculation as to whether he was hired by the Soviets to kill Kennedy.

If Oswald did kill Kennedy, he didn't do a very good job of covering his tracks. Eyewitnesses informed police they believed the shots to have been fired from Texas School Book Depository Building where, on the sixth floor behind some boxes, they quickly discovered a Mannlicher-Carcano bolt-action rifle and three used cartridges. The gun was registered to 'A. Hidell', a name used by Oswald, a twenty-three-year-old shipping clerk employed by the Book Depository.

Kennedy wasn't the only man to lose his life in Dallas that sunny November day. Approximately forty-five minutes later, Police officer, J. D. Tippit was shot while on patrol in the Oak

Cliff residential community of Dallas, a neighbourhood south-west of the site where Kennedy was shot. Eyewitnesses would later identify Oswald as the killer in line-ups, but testimony varied considerably about the time, actions and number of people involved in Tippit's death. Half an hour after Tippit's death, fifteen police officers stormed the Texas Theatre in Oak Cliff where a man had entered the theatre without paying. There they apprehended and arrested Lee Harvey Oswald for Tippit's murder. He was charged with Kennedy's murder the following day.

Motives

If the lone gunman theory endorsed by the US Government and put forward in the findings of the Warren Commission Report (a committee chaired by chief justice Earl Warren, the aim of which was to investigate the FBI reports and interview witnesses, to put to bed any conspiracy rumours about Kennedy's assassination) is to be believed, then Lee Harvey Oswald acted alone, and had his own reasons for gunning down the president. The Warren Report painted Oswald as one of life's losers, a loner who had been involved in petty crime, and a vehement supporter of radical left-wing politics. His connections to these left-wing groups and his associations with Cuban and Soviet government personnel were downplayed, while the image of him as a madman, possessed by pathological oddities and extreme views, was emphasised. Oswald denied killing Kennedy, so no reason was ever given by him for why he may have shot the president, but, if he did act alone, there is good evidence to suggest that his political motives, combined with his military training, made him capable and culpable of the crime.

Aftermath

The days after President Kennedy was shot played out like a tragic Hollywood film, as Americans all over the country stayed glued to the news broadcasts on the nearest television set. Everything had happened in quick succession: the assassination, the arrest of a suspect, said suspect being charged. Oswald was then to be transported from the police station where he had been detained, to the county jail. A police tip-off ensured that a huge crowd had gathered, including a large number of photographers and journalists. Live news broadcasts showed footage of Oswald being led through the police station basement, when a man stepped forward and shot Oswald in the stomach. A scuffle ensued between the police, the attacker and the press, while news reports flooded in that Oswald had been shot by an unknown assailant. An ambulance arrived to take Oswald to Parkland Hospital where President Kennedy had been taken the day before. He died shortly afterwards. The man who shot Oswald was Jack Rubenstein, known as Jack Ruby, a nightclub owner originally from Chicago, who was known for his connections to both the Mob and the police. Ruby was convicted of Oswald's murder in 1964, but less than three years later, while appealing his conviction, he died of lung cancer at Parkland Hospital.

President Kennedy was given a full state funeral three days after the assassination on 25 November 1963, at St Matthew's Cathedral in Washington DC. The funeral was broadcast around the world, and the sight of a veiled Jacqueline Kennedy with her two young children by her side remains one of the iconic images of the 1960s. Unfortunately for the Kennedy family, the debate about and investigation into what had happened over the preceding five days didn't end with JFK's burial. The search for 'the truth' would continue for many years to come (see below). Some still believe that Oswald was a scapegoat for a wider conspiracy involving those in the highest positions of power.

The truth is out there...

If the public trusted the government before Kennedy's death, then the events that followed had many people questioning whether what they were being told was true. Around the time of the assassination, only 29 per cent of Americans thought that Oswald had acted alone. The differing reports of witnesses and journalists led to suggestions of a cover-up, and very soon any new evidence was being analysed by the public with a sceptical mind. The government's speedy arrest and charge of Oswald, Oswald's death and the findings of the Warren Commission did nothing to quash the circulating conspiracy theories that Kennedy had been killed on orders from Russians, Cubans, the CIA, the American Mafia and even President Lyndon B. Johnson. Here are some of the factors that fuelled those conspiracies, which many still believe to be true.

— The Warren Report, published on 24 September 1964, supported the original theory that Oswald had acted alone in his plan to kill Kennedy. Three spent cartridges were found at the Book Depository where the murder weapon was located, but eyewitness testimony, including that of Governor Connally's wife, referred to the noise of a fourth shot. This was later supported by the findings of the 1970s House Select Committee on Assassinations, which used audio evidence from one of the motorcade's motorcycle radios to prove that four shots were fired. This evidence was later disputed, with Dealey Plaza being referred to as an echo chamber that could have distorted the sounds of the three shots.

— Oswald was a trained Marine and, according to his military records, was proficient with firearms, but despite the Warren Report's claims, many still believed it would have been impossible for him to fire three rounds from the 1938 Mannlicher-Carcano in the 5.6-second time frame in which the shots were fired. In 1967, CBS sponsored a test to learn if it was indeed possible. Ballistics expert Howard Donahue was able to hit a moving target from over 200m away three times in under 5.6 seconds, proving that it could be done.

— The report from Kennedy's hurried autopsy, carried out under great pressure and stress, contained a number of inaccuracies, which led people to be suspicious. While it's likely that such inaccuracies were simply a result of human error, exacerbated by the pressure to produce a result, the unknown whereabouts of Kennedy's brain and the apparent cover-up and ordered silencing of autopsy witnesses by the government, has led many to believe an impartial autopsy would have revealed details about the bullets' trajectories that may have revealed a second shooter was involved. The initial report described the wound to Kennedy's throat as similar to an entry wound. The building Oswald supposedly fired from was positioned behind the president at the time of the attack, so this information supported many people's claims that there had been a second shooter, positioned towards the front of the motorcade. The autopsy data has since been examined and this evidence has been refuted. The 'entry wound' is believed by many to be an exit wound, given that there was no exit wound at the back of Kennedy's head. Expert Donahue believes the trajectory of the head wound bullet actually came from a horizontal angle from behind the president, and not from the high vantage point of the School Book Depository building.

He has pointed the finger at the Secret Service agents in the car following the president's, citing an accidental discharge as the reason for the fatal shot. Regardless, the lack of professional etiquette displayed during the autopsy meant the future gathering of reliable forensic evidence was nearly impossible.

— Jack Ruby said he killed Lee Harvey Oswald to spare Jacqueline Kennedy's feelings, but the ease with which he was able to bring down a man who should have been the most highly guarded prisoner in the United States at that time, and the staged nature of Oswald's death, reeks of a set-up and, together with Ruby's Mob and police connections, led many to believe that someone wanted Oswald silenced before the truth could come out in court.

The grassy knoll

The famous 'grassy knoll' refers to the raised lawn area that lined the north side of Elm Street in Dealey Plaza. Zapruder's iconic film of the assassination was taken from the grassy knoll and many witnesses claimed to have heard gunshots coming from that area, leading to the conspiracies that Oswald was not the only person with crosshairs on the president that day. In the aftermath of the shooting, some people ran in the direction of the knoll, believing that was where the shot had come from. They were reportedly turned back by a Secret Service agent. The audio evidence that formed the basis of the assumption by the 1970s House Select Committee on Assassinations that there was more than one shooter, indicated that the second assassin was situated on the grassy knoll.

Zapruder's film

Perhaps surprisingly, the only video footage of the event, Zapruder's film, was not broadcast in its entirety until 1975, some twelve years after the assassination. While the Secret Service had homed in on Zapruder an hour after Kennedy was shot, and made two copies of the film, and news agencies bid to release the footage, it was decided that the content was too graphic for audiences at the time. *LIFE* magazine secured an exclusive deal to print frames from the film in their 29 November 1963 edition, but only thirty frames appeared in print. When the film was finally aired on *Good Night America*, sensitive viewers were told to switch over to the late-night movie, and commentators disputed the findings of the Warren Report, which had been published over a decade previously.

The man who didn't kill Kennedy

If it hadn't been for President Kennedy's love of photo opportunities, or the recent birth of his son John F. Kennedy Jr., he may have been brought down by a lone killer a lot sooner than 1963. After winning the presidential election in November 1960, JFK spent his time travelling between his family's various residences while he put his cabinet together. As the president-elect, he would not be inaugurated until 20 January 1961. A retired postal worker from New Hampshire named Richard P. Pavlick was unhappy about Kennedy winning the election and felt that it had been bought for him by his father Joe Kennedy. Pavlick had a history of psychiatric problems and was known for voicing his ire about Kennedy's election in letters to local newspapers. He sold or gave away everything he owned and, at some point in December, made his way to Florida where Kennedy was staying at the family's Palm Beach house. He had built a bomb in his car and his plan was to wait for JFK to emerge from the house and head to his car, and then Pavlick would drive into Kennedy's limousine, so detonating the bomb and killing himself and the president-elect.

Seventy-three-year-old Pavlick's plan was thwarted by Kennedy's desire for positive media attention. Every time he left the house to make his way to the car, he was surrounded by photographers, and was therefore routinely accompanied by his wife and their new-born son, John Jr. Consequently Pavlick could not bring himself to needlessly kill Jacqueline or the baby, and parked in the road for five days in the hope of catching Kennedy on his own. Rather fortuitously, he was arrested by a Palm Beach police officer for a minor traffic violation. His explosive device was then found and he was charged with attempting to assassinate the president-elect on 16 December 1960. The Secret Service initially denied that Pavlick had come close to killing Kennedy, but a week after Kennedy's inauguration, a retiring Secret Service chief changed his tune, admitting to the danger Pavlick had posed to the new president.

The other Kennedy

The moving images of JFK's assassination in 1963 will forever eclipse the footage of the assassination of his younger brother, Robert, some five years later. John Kennedy was the president, and while he wasn't widely popular at the time of his death, the sight of him being shot in the head, with his glamorous wife by his side, was sickening and shocking to the whole country, even to those who opposed his decisions in office. His brother, however, was a fresh hope, a New York senator vying for the Democratic nomination for the 1968 presidential elections. Robert, or Bobby as he was more commonly known, had helped his brother win the presidency, but was as yet unproved in the political arena on his own. There was much anticipation on 4 June 1968 as to whether he would win the California presidential primary and be one step closer to the nomination and his own chance at the White House.

Unfortunately, that dream was never to become reality. Tension was running high that summer. Martin Luther King Jr. had been killed just two months before and the country was abuzz with civil rights issues, revolutionary politics and the fighting in Vietnam. But although Kennedy was aware his life could be in danger throughout the campaign, as he waited for the results of the Californian primaries in the Ambassador Hotel in Los Angeles, security was relaxed and there was excitement, not concern, in the air.

At 11.40 that night, the news came in that Kennedy had won the vote and he delivered a speech in the Embassy Ballroom to his supporters and campaign staff, who had gathered for the celebration. At 12.15 on the morning on 5 June, the senator made his way through the ballroom and headed to the Colonial Room for a press conference. He chose to walk through the crowded hotel kitchen, where a man named Sirhan Sirhan stepped towards Kennedy and with a .22 calibre pistol, shot him in the head, chest and neck. Five other people were shot in the fracas that followed as people tried to disarm Sirhan. After three hours of surgery, a chance of recovery seemed possible, but Kennedy took a turn for the worse and died in the early hours of 6 June.

Many witnesses had seen Kennedy's assassin shoot him point-blank, but the reason why the twenty-four-year-old Palestinian immigrant killed the senator emerged when his room was searched and notebooks containing his plan to kill Kennedy were discovered. His main motivation was Kennedy's pro-Israeli stance on the situation in the Middle East, and he was especially angered by American politicians who celebrated Israel's victory in the Six-Day War of 1967. Sirhan pleaded not guilty, and has maintained ever since that he has no recollection of the assassination or his confession or the trial. He was originally found guilty and sentenced to death, but three years later, his sentence was reduced to life imprisonment due to the death penalty being outlawed in 1972. He is still serving his life sentence in a Californian prison.

Failed assassin

Name: Samuel J. Byck.

Profile: Byck, aged forty-four, was a former tyre salesman who was unemployed at the time of the attempt. Byck had been married and was a father of four children. But, unhappy family life and the struggle to find work had led to psychiatric problems including depression. He came to the attention of the Secret Service a few years prior to his assassination attempt, after he openly threatened President Nixon's life in 1972. Testimony from Byck's psychiatrist had persuaded the district attorney to drop the investigation. Later, it was discovered that the Christmas prior to his assassination attempt, he had been arrested for protesting in front of the White House without a permit and had also protested there wearing a Santa Claus costume.

Target: President Richard Nixon.

Motive: Byck blamed those in power for his problems and resented the 'corrupt' authorities, including the government. After his application for a loan was rejected by the Small Business Administration, he focused his attentions and anger on Nixon as a figurehead of all that was wrong in his world and began planning to assassinate him.

Time of attack: 7.15 a.m., 22 February 1974.

Location: Baltimore-Washington International Airport, aboard DC-9 Delta Airlines Flight 523 to Atlanta. The assassination of Nixon was planned to take place at the White House, but the plane never left the airport.

Plan of action: Byck had carefully thought out how he would kill Nixon and recorded his plan on a cassette tape which he mailed to *Washington Post* columnist Jack Anderson, hours before he set his plan in motion. He named his plan Operation Pandora's Box, and described how he would hijack a plane and fly it towards his target area, Washington DC. Once the White House was in sight, he planned to shoot the pilot dead and fly the plane into building, killing himself, all the passengers and anyone in the White House.

What happened next: That morning, as planned, Byck walked through the airport and pulled out his revolver, shot a security guard in the back, leapt over the security check and boarded the Atlanta flight. Once on board, he forced his way into the cockpit, killed one of the pilots and wounded the other. After ordering the pilot to take off, he was informed the flight could not leave without the wheel blocks being removed. He repeatedly shot the pilots and even grabbed a nearby passenger shouting at her to fly the plane. He was then wounded by police bullets and, before the authorities could get to him, he shot himself in the head. Police found a gasoline bomb in a briefcase under his body.

Aftermath: While that day ended a little differently from the way Byck had planned it, Richard Nixon wouldn't stay in the White House for long. Less than six months later, on 9 August 1974, he resigned from the presidency over the Watergate scandal.

Lucky escape: Gerald Ford (1913-2006)

While Mary Surratt was the first woman to be sentenced to death and hanged for her alleged involvement in a presidential assassination, only two women have tried to kill a US president, and they both had their sights set on the same one. Gerald Ford was the target of these two assassination attempts in the autumn of 1975, just weeks apart. The first took place on 5 September 1975 in Sacramento, California. At 9.55 a.m., right on schedule, President Ford left the Senator Hotel in downtown Sacramento and began the short one-block walk to the Capitol building, where he had a 10 a.m. meeting with Governor Jerry Brown. He was surrounded by the usual number of Secret Service agents (the actual number is kept secret) as he made his way across the park in front of the Capitol building, and was met by applause from the waiting crowd, who hoped to catch a glimpse of their president or shake his hand. While greeting the crowd near a magnolia tree, Ford noticed a lady dressed in red in the front row raise her hand, as if to be greeted. He momentarily froze when he realised she was holding a revolver barely 60cm from his face. She cried out, 'The country is in a mess! This man is not your president!' The gun didn't fire (there was no bullet in the chamber that was ready to be fired, although there were four bullets loaded in the gun), and Secret Service Agent Larry Buendorf lunged at her almost immediately, snatching the gun from her grasp and handcuffing her. The president was unharmed and escorted directly into the Capitol by other agents, where he regained his composure and had his meeting with the governor, without mentioning the incident.

The wannabe assassin was Lynette Alice Fromme, known as Squeaky Fromme, a dedicated follower of Charles Manson, who had been imprisoned for his involvement in the Sharon

Tate killings in 1969, and a member of the Manson 'family'. She hoped to bring attention to Manson's defence by shooting Ford, and had told a journalist earlier in the year that Ford was following in Nixon's footsteps of lying to the American people. She also said that something very big was going to happen, perhaps an indication that the assassination was planned far in advance. Some believe Manson himself may have been involved in the conspiracy to kill Ford, as he regularly communicated with his followers, including Fromme, from prison.

Seventeen days later, outside the St Francis Hotel in San Francisco, another woman had a go at killing President Ford; her name was Sara Jane Moore. She was a left-wing activist who sometimes acted as an informant for the FBI. This time, despite standing at least twelve metres away, the assassin managed to fire a shot as Ford greeted the crowd. Experts believe that, had Moore been firing her own more powerful .44 Magnum, which had recently been confiscated by police, she would have had a much greater chance of hitting the president. Luckily, the bullet missed Ford's head and ricocheted off the side of the hotel, injuring a taxi driver. Fromme and Moore served thirty-four and thirty-two years of their life sentences respectively, and were released on parole in 2009 and 2007.

Lucky escape: Ronald Reagan (1911-2004)

There are very few presidents who have been shot while in office and survived to tell the tale. Ronald Reagan is one of them. The attempt on Reagan's life on 30 March 1981 is also distinct because it is the rarer example of an assassination plot of a famous political figure for non-political means. John Hinckley Jr. wasn't even sure if he wanted to kill himself or a president, and he certainly didn't give much regard to which one. Reagan later described Hinckley as being from a 'fine family' and, as the son of an oil executive who was known to the Bush family, he would have seemed an unlikely candidate for the role of assassin. Leading up to his attempt on Reagan's life, Hinckley was seeing a psychiatrist and taking anti-depressants. The year prior to the Reagan attack, he was caught in Nashville, Tennessee, with guns in his bag, on a day when President Jimmy Carter was in town. Hinckley's motives for killing such a high-profile figure stemmed from his infatuation with film actress Jodie Foster, since watching her repeatedly in the 1976 film *Taxi Driver*. Foster was a student at Yale University at the time, and Hinckley had enrolled in classes there and sent letters and poems to the actress in the hope of attracting her attention. With no success, he became convinced that the notoriety associated with an assassination would make him Foster's equal and improve his chances.

He also considered committing suicide. On the day Hinckley struck, Reagan had been at the Hilton Hotel in Washington DC to deliver a speech to a labour union conference. A small crowd had gathered outside the hotel as Reagan left and made his way to the limousine that awaited him. He was close to the car when Hinckley, who was in the crowd, crouched down and opened fire. Secret Service Agent Tim McCarthy tried to block the line of fire between Hinckley and Reagan, while another agent bundled the president into the back of the car, unaware he had been shot. The next few minutes were chaotic as Secret Service agents restrained Hinckley, who was still trying to fire his gun despite having unloaded all its bullets. Other than Reagan, three men had been shot: McCarthy, a police officer named Tom Delhanty and Reagan's press secretary, James Brady. Brady's injuries were the most severe, as the bullet was lodged in the right side of his brain, and he was left brain damaged and partially paralysed.

Reagan, meanwhile, was rushed to George Washington University Hospital, where it was discovered a bullet had lodged in his left lung, 2.5cm from his heart. He was operated on and made a full recovery. Hinckley was found not guilty by reason of insanity during his 1982 trial for thirteen crimes, including the attempt on Reagan's life. He was detained in St Elizabeth's Hospital in Washington where he still resides. In 2009, he was granted permission for extended conditional visits to see his mother away from the psychiatric hospital, and further visits were granted in 2011.

Changing the law

The public were outraged when Hinckley was found not guilty on all thirteen counts in court, despite numerous witnesses, and photo and video evidence of his crimes. Immediately following the Hinckley trial, Congress began debating the insanity defence and its usage. The outcome was a fundamental change of law, proposed by Senator Arlen Specter, which suggested that, rather than the prosecution having to prove the defendant's sanity, it should be the defence counsel's responsibility to prove their client to be insane. Three years after the trial, two-thirds of the US states had followed the example of Congress and applied the proof of insanity measure, while Utah completely abolished the use of an insanity defence. This change in the law was not the only outcome of the Hinckley trial. James Brady and his wife Sarah became high-profile campaigners for stricter gun control laws, which ultimately resulted in the Brady Act (1994), a law that required background checks for people purchasing firearms.

Unsolved: Olof Palme (1927-86)

On 28 February 1986, Sweden's Prime Minister Olof Palme took the subway to the centre of Stockholm with his wife Lisbet, to meet their son and his partner for a trip to the cinema. After they watched the movie, the two couples went their separate ways. About five minutes later, at 11.21 p.m., as the prime minister and his wife were making their way to the subway station, a man came from behind and shot the Swedish leader twice in the back. His wife turned and caught sight of the assailant, whose features were obscured by his dark coat and a cap covering much of his face. He fired at her but missed, and then ran away into the night. There was no saving Palme — the wounds killed him within minutes of the attack.

The assassination remains one of Sweden's great unsolved crimes, twenty-five years after it occurred. The police response in the immediate aftermath of the attack is largely blamed for the lack of physical evidence retrieved from the crime scene and the assassin being able to make an unimpeded getaway. That's not to say the police haven't thoroughly investigated the crime in the decades since: huge amounts of money have been spent on the case and a number of individuals and groups have had the finger pointed at them.

Viktor Gunnarsson: As a Swedish extremist and member of a number of right-wing groups, including a branch of the LaRoche movement, Gunnarsson was the first suspect in the Palme case, as witnesses had placed him at the scene of the crime. He was included in a botched police line-up, but with no concrete evidence to hold him, he was released without charge.

Kurdish Workers' Party: Not long after the murder, thirteen Kurds living in Sweden were taken into custody, but were then released without charge. Police suspected that a left-wing Kurdish group may have been involved in the assassination, but despite these arrests, the suspicions led to nothing. In 2001, investigators visited an island prison to interview a Kurdish rebel leader named Abdullah Ocalan, about allegations he made that a dissident Kurdish group had assassinated Palme. These claims have not led to any charges.

Gustav Christer Petterson: Petterson remains the only person charged with the murder of Olof Palme. He was arrested nearly two years after the shooting, and, while he had a previous murder conviction and had spent much of his life incarcerated in prisons and psychiatric hospitals, there was no forensic evidence to pin him to the crime scene, no motive and no murder weapon. He was largely convicted because Palme's wife picked him out in a line-up. His conviction was overturned a year later and he was freed, on the grounds that identifying him two years after the crime was not evidence enough for the conviction. Petterson died in 2004.

South African Secret Police: Olof Palme supported the antiapartheid movement in South Africa and many believe that the South African Secret Police sent an assassin to kill him, to stop secret Swedish payments being made to the African National Congress. The former head of that police operation, Eugene de Kock, claimed in court that this was the case, and that the shooting had been orchestrated by a known enemy of his, named Craig Williamson. Swedish investigators were unable to find enough evidence to support these allegations.

Iron ladies

Over the last thirty years, as more and more women have found a voice in the political sphere, a number of high-profile female politicians have had to face the threat of assassination, and in some cases, the real-life horror of an attempt on their life. Maybe their rarity in politics has made these women more determined to forge ahead with their work and to not succumb to the scaremongering tactics of their attackers, but, gender aside, there's no denying the courage and commitment to their political positions all these women have shown in the face of true danger.

Margaret Thatcher (1925-2013): One of the most notable female leaders of the twentieth century was Margaret Thatcher, and, despite her reputation as the unshakeable Iron Lady, and insistence on tight security for herself, leading British politicians and the royal family, even she was not above the tactics of a group of deadly IRA members who plotted to eliminate her. The attack took place at 2.54 a.m. on 12 October 1984, at the Grand Hotel in Brighton, where Thatcher and other Conservative Party officials were staying for the party's annual conference. A bomb went off inside the hotel, causing one side of the building to collapse, including the bathroom adjoining Thatcher's room, which she had just used. While she was unharmed, more than thirty people were injured in the blast and four died. The bomb had been planted by an IRA explosives expert called Patrick Magee, who had checked into the hotel three weeks before the conference, to set the timer. Magee and three accomplices were arrested and charged eight months later. They had made detailed plans to detonate a number of other bombs targeting high-profile individuals, including the Queen Mother.

Indira Gandhi (1917-84): When Patrick Magee headed to the Grand Hotel in Brighton with the intention of killing Margaret Thatcher, it was only a few weeks before Indian Prime Minister Indira Gandhi was shot to death. While Thatcher's uncompromising approach to the situation in Northern Ireland, and her decisions regarding treatment of IRA prisoners, caused the group's rising anger towards her, Gandhi became a hate figure for some of the Sikh population after ordering the Indian army to occupy one of the faith's holiest temples, which had become a stronghold for a group of militant Sikh separatists campaigning for the creation of a Sikh homeland. During the occupation of the temple, 1,000 people were killed, and anger among the Sikh community rose. Gandhi was shot dead by two of her own guards on the morning of 31 October 1984 as she left her home for a TV interview recording. The two Sikh men, Beant Singh and Satwant Singh, hit her with a dozen bullets between them. Her death led to vicious mob attacks on the Sikh community. Gandhi's son Rajiv succeeded her as prime minister but was assassinated himself seven years later by a Tamil Tiger guerrilla fighter in a suicide bomb attack which left him, Gandhi and sixteen bystanders dead.

Anna Lindh (1957-2003): Swedish Foreign Minister Lindh was shopping in a luxury department store on 10 September 2003 when she was stabbed repeatedly in a violent and frenzied attack by Mijailo Mijailovic. The politician, who was spearheading the government's campaign to encourage citizens to choose the Euro in the upcoming referendum on the currency, died in hospital the next morning after surgeons were unable to save her. Although police initially believed Lindh was the victim of an extreme right-wing assassination, her twenty-five-year-old Swedish murderer would later claim voices in his head told him to attack her. In court, the prosecution tried to argue he had followed her, and that Lindh had been targeted because of her powerful political position. Mijailovic was sentenced to life in prison.

Benazir Bhutto (1953-2007): Former Pakistani Prime Minister Bhutto survived a terrifying assassination attempt on 18 October 2007, a few months before she was killed by a suicide bomber in Rawalpindi, Pakistan, on 27 December. She had been in self-imposed exile for eight years after being charged with corruption in 1999, and, in October 2007, she was returning to her homeland in the hopes of being re-elected as the new prime minister. She arrived at Jinnah International airport, where she was greeted by thousands of supporters and a convoy, including a specially designed bulletproof vehicle. Nearly twelve hours after her arrival in Karachi — it took nearly three hours for Bhutto to make the 100-metre journey out of the airport because of the crowds — two explosions that went off near Bhutto's vehicle, resulted in a final death toll of 139 and injured about 450 people. Bhutto remained unharmed, but that December, she was attacked again while campaigning for provincial and parliamentary elections. The former prime minister was riding in an armoured vehicle and was standing up and waving to the crowds through the vehicle's roof hatch. A Scotland Yard investigation into her death confirmed the Pakistani government's official line that, although a man had opened fire on Bhutto's car, it was the detonation of a suicide bomb a few seconds later that caused her death.

Gabrielle Giffords (1970-): In 2011, US Representative Gabrielle Giffords was conducting a 'Congress on your corner' session with members of her congressional district in a supermarket car park in Tucson, Arizona, when a man shot her in the head at point-blank range, and then opened fire on the crowd. Six people were killed in the 8 January attack, including a federal judge and a nine-year-old girl, while thirteen others were injured. Giffords survived her injuries after intensive medical attention and rehabilitation. Police arrested and charged a suspect named Jared Lee Loughner, but, in May 2011, a judge deemed him incompetent to stand trial based on initial mental evaluations carried out by court-appointed experts. If he does eventually stand trial, he could face the death penalty.

Chapter Six: A Bad Attempt

The scale of the outrage in which we have all shared, and the fact that we are gathered here now ... is a sign not only that this attack has failed, but that all attempts to destroy democracy by terrorism will fail
Margaret Thatcher

The high-profile deaths chronicled in this book depict how far individuals, organisations and even governments will go to make a political statement and essentially change the course of history. Often, as we have seen, their goals are not achieved, and while government policies, politicians and practices are usually affected by the assassination, the changes made after the fact are rarely those that the assassins hoped for. Over the course of history, there have been a number of public figures who have survived an attempt on their life (some more than once), leading us to question how history might have been shaped had the perpetrators been successful: shot slightly to the left, detonated the bomb a little sooner, come up with a feasible plan (see Fidel Castro). However poorly thought through or badly executed the attempt, there is no denying that many of the victims in this chapter were the recipients of some skilled medical care and a good dose of old-fashioned luck. History has shown that, no matter whether you're the Queen of England or a murderous dictator, you could be the target of an assassination plot, but whether you survive is often left to bad timing, poor planning and/or a twist of fate.

Napoleon Bonaparte (1769-1821)

A number of attempts were made on the life of Napoleon Bonaparte during his years in power. As the first consul of the French Republic, Bonaparte was the most powerful man in France and he had many enemies, including royalists who wanted to see the monarchy reinstated. There were reports of plots to kidnap him, or to kill him by switching his snuff box with one laced with poison. An alleged plot to attack Bonaparte as he left the opera house in October 1800, came to the attention of those closest to him, and they set a trap to prevent the assassins carrying out their plan — although the truth behind the plot and the assassins involved have been questioned — and four of them were sentenced to death. A couple of months later, on Christmas Eve, Bonaparte left his residence at the Tuileries Palace in Paris on his way to the opera. When a horse and cart appeared to be blocking the way of Napoleon's carriage on the Rue Saint-Nicaise, rather than slow down to wait for it to pass, Napoleon's coachman, who was reportedly drunk, speeded up and squeezed through the small space. A few moments later, the cart exploded, killing approximately nine people (although reports differ on this) and injuring many more. Napoleon was unharmed and arrived at the opera house to rapturous applause. The plot was arranged by royalists who had not anticipated the speed of Napoleon's carriage, or the poor quality of the gunpowder, which exploded too late. This, compounded by a later plot to kill the first consul in 1804, organised by the ousted royal family, indirectly led to Napoleon creating a new hereditary monarchy, with himself as the first Emperor of France.

Queen Victoria (1819-1901)

'It is worth being shot at — to see how much one is loved', wrote Queen Victoria to one of her daughters about the 1882 attempt to assassinate her. The fact the monarch could write so flippantly about what could have been the end of her reign, and her life at the age of sixty-two, probably had a lot to do with the fact that she was not fully aware she was under attack until after the fact. It was on 2 March 1882 that Queen Victoria boarded a train from London to Windsor and, on exiting the train station, was picked up by a carriage to travel the final leg of the journey to Windsor Castle. As they began to leave, the queen's daughter, Princess Beatrice, who was seated by the carriage window, saw a man step forward and fire a revolver directly at them. He was promptly set upon by a group of boys from Eton school, who were less than impressed to see their monarch under fire. It was only then, noticing the kerfuffle going on outside, that Queen Victoria asked her servant, John Brown, what was happening. Luckily, the Queen was unharmed, but the fact she had cheated death improved public opinion of her significantly. The man holding the revolver was Roderick Maclean, a Scot suffering from mental illness — he had spent time in lunatic asylums — and who fancied himself as a poet. He had previously sent a poem to the queen, to which he received a reply saying that the queen did not read manuscript poetry. At the trial, he was found not guilty and sent back to a mental hospital.

Maclean was not the only man to be confined to a mental hospital for trying to kill the queen. Forty-two years earlier, in 1840, when Victoria was just twenty-one-years-old, the pregnant monarch was riding with her husband Prince Albert in an open-top carriage from Buckingham Palace up Constitution Hill, when a man wielding two pistols leapt forward and fired twice at the royal couple. During the trial, a witness testified that Queen Victoria had tried to rise up from a crouching position after the first pistol was fired, just missing the top of her head, and that Albert had pushed her down before the second shot rang out, narrowly missing her. Neither of the two royals were injured by the would-be assassin, Edward Oxford, who worked as a barman. While Oxford was found guilty of high treason, he did not face the gallows and was imprisoned in an asylum, where he stayed for twenty-seven years.

Adolf Hitler (1889-1945)

The elimination of world leaders, policy makers and dictators by minority groups and individuals, can have a dramatic impact on the governance and political agenda of a country in the aftermath. Although, more often than not, a similar successor is ready to step into the victim's shoes. In the case of Nazi Germany's leader Adolf Hitler, it was some of his closest allies who decided, in 1944, to try and bring about his death, despite the huge risk to their own lives. Towards the end of World War Two, a number of senior German officers were angry at where the country was heading, and strongly opposed the killings and mass extermination of people that Hitler's policies demanded. It was the German surrender at the Battle of Stalingrad, where the German army and their allies were finally defeated by the Soviets, that made a number of Germans certain that Hitler's leadership was bad for the country, and that, if a new government wasn't put in place, Germany might find itself under Soviet rule.

The most famous plot, known as Operation Valkyrie, centred upon the assassination of Hitler and the start of a military *coup*, which planned to see Ludwig Beck, an army general and the chief of the German General Staff, replace Hitler as head of state and lead a military government. Hitler's death was seen as necessary to convince other senior officials that a military takeover would be a success. For a plan to assassinate one of the most powerful men in Europe, it was relatively simple. The reserve army's Chief of Staff, Colonel Claus Schenk von Stauffenberg, supported the *coup* and was in a good strategic position to know the Führer's whereabouts, as he attended meetings at the dictator's hideout in Rastenburg, East Prussia. It was at one of these meetings, in a wooden building, that Stauffenberg and his fellow conspirator Lieutenant Werner von Haeften, planned to blow up the Nazi leader.

On 20 July 1944, the two men arrived and were waved through the gates of the headquarters without being searched. Had any of the guards had the nerve to search Stauffenberg's briefcase, they would have found two devices attached to plastic explosives. After a briefing with some other senior Nazi officers, the two men retired to the bathroom, locked the door and started setting the timers on the devices, but they were interrupted. To avoid arousing suspicion, Stauffenberg emerged from the bathroom with only one of the bombs primed and ready in his briefcase, while the other stayed in Haeften's bag.

In the meeting, Stauffenberg took his seat to the right of Hitler at a large oak table. He placed the briefcase under the table, resting it against a table leg. Shortly after, he made his excuses and left the meeting. At 12.45 p.m., as Hitler perused a map, the bomb exploded, destroying the hut and causing fatal injuries to four men, including a stenographer who had his legs blown off. Hitler, however, survived relatively unscathed with shattered eardrums, splinters and burns. He would continue business as usual that day, meeting with Italian fascist leader Benito Mussolini.

As far as Stauffenberg and Haeften were concerned, the explosion they heard from a nearby airfield, as they waited to board a plane to head back to Berlin, was evidence of Hitler's death. Believing there was no chance he had survived the explosion, the two men arrived in Berlin with the news that the Führer was dead, and Beck declared himself the new German leader. That evening, Nazi propagandist Joseph Goebbels made a radio broadcast informing the German people, and the conspirators, that Hitler was alive and well. The plan had failed and the band of plotters knew a terrible fate awaited them. Stauffenberg's superior gave Beck the opportunity to kill himself, but did not offer the same end to Stauffenberg and Haeften, who were shot in a courtyard. Arguably, this was a more humane end than the execution Hitler had in mind, and indeed ordered, for others who were believed to be involved in the conspiracy. A number of those involved in the plot were hung up by meat hooks, with piano wire around their necks to face slow and excruciating deaths.

How Hitler survived

— The July 1944 bombing of the wooden building where Hitler was meeting was not the only plot to kill the Führer. Rather surprisingly, the only attempts carried out were those planned by German natives.

— Other than the 1944 attempt, the closest Hitler came to losing his life at the hands of an assassin was in November 1939. Every year, Hitler attended the annual commemorative celebrations of the Beer Hall Putsch in Munich, where the

Nazi Party had tried to start a revolutionary *coup* in 1923. This year was no different, except that a carpenter named George Elser had spent nearly a whole year working as a renovator at the beer hall while he built a bomb to blow up the Führer. The device, which contained 50kg of explosives, was capable of being set up to six days in advance and was installed in the pillar behind the podium from which Hitler would deliver his speech. Elser set the bomb to go off at 9.20 p.m. on 9 November, when he believed Hitler would be speaking to the audience gathered in the beer hall, and he then fled to the Swiss border. As predicted, Hitler delivered his speech on time but, for some unknown reason, cut it short and left the event. It was only a few minutes later, when his fleet of vehicles reached the station, that the bomb exploded, killing eight people and injuring more than sixty others. Hitler and his closest advisers were unharmed, and the party's newspaper blamed the bombing on British Secret Service agents. Elser was picked up at the Swiss border and spent the next six years in concentration camps. It is believed he was executed in April 1945, a few weeks before the Führer took his own life, but the Nazis claimed he was killed in an allied bombing raid.

— The German officers led by General Ludwig Beck, tried to assassinate Hitler a number of times in 1943 before the most famous 1944 attempt. These included a bomb disguised as a bottle of brandy, which was put on board Hitler's plane but failed to go off, and a failed suicide bomber named Colonel von Gersdorff, who walked around an exhibition hall with Hitler, with two bombs under his coat, but was unable to detonate the bombs before Hitler left.

— The Germans weren't the only people coming up with plans to kill Hitler. A British organisation known as the Special Operations Executive (SOE), that liaised with resistance fighters across Europe, was asked to come up with a number of methods to assassinate the Führer in the summer of 1944. While there was strong opposition to assassinating Hitler, because his tactical military errors were actually aiding the Allied war effort, it was felt that the war was being continued because of his personal ambitions, and that eliminating the dictator could effectually end the war. The SOE's plans to take out Hitler included: bombarding his Bavarian retreat near Berchtesgaden, followed by a parachute assault to ensure Hitler had been killed by the bombing; a lone sniper shooting Hitler as he took his morning walk; and a number of plans involving the dictator's personal train, the Führerzug, such as poisoning the train's supply of drinking water and derailing the train inside a tunnel. These and other outlandish ideas, such as poison-filled fountain pen syringes and contaminating Hitler's clothes, were never carried out.

Charles de Gaulle (1890-1970)

The Frenchman survived a rather startling thirty-one attempts on his life during his time in office, serving between 1944 and 1966 as the leader of the Free French movement, the prime minister and the president of France. While he was a controversial figure during World War Two, for allying France with the British and refusing to bow to Nazi rule, it was during and after the Algerian War (1954-62) that Charles de Gaulle found his life most at risk from the military personnel and refugee French-Algerians, who saw his decision to give Algeria independence as defeatist.

Many of the hits targeting de Gaulle were carried out under the direction of a group called Organisation de l'Armée Secrète (OAS). While others had tried to kill de Gaulle in the past, the first serious attempt by the OAS took place on 8 September 1961, while the president was travelling with his wife from Paris to his country home in Colombey-les-Deux-Eglises. The OAS had hidden plastic explosives and a canister of napalm at the roadside, outside the village of Crancey. When the president's car approached, a device exploded, veering the car to the left, and the napalm produced a fireball that blasted across the road. De Gaulle urged his driver to keep going through the fire and to safety. The only real damage done was to one of the car's headlights.

But the OAS wasn't through yet, and less than a year later, on 22 August 1962, they struck again when the president and his wife were being driven home by the same driver. The OAS was able to gain information from a contact in the presidential palace about de Gaulle's itinerary and in which car he would be driven. Fifteen men were involved in the plot, led by Colonel Jean Bastien-Thiry, which saw them wait in parked cars packed with weapons on a street in the outskirts of Paris. The colonel stood at a bus stop, ready to signal to his collaborators to block the road with one of the cars when he saw the president approach. Events didn't play out as they had planned, though: when Bastien-Thiry's men failed to see his signal, there was no time to block the road and, in a disorganised panic, the men began firing at the car with machine guns. The heavily armed men were able to blow out the tyres on de Gaulle's car, and then gave chase, firing at the car as the president's skilled driver tried to escape from the onslaught. Eventually, the assassins gave up their pursuit, but not without causing a significant amount of damage to the president's car, which was hit by six bullets. The only injury to its passengers was a cut to de Gaulle's arm caused by shattered window glass.

The severe threat of the OAS was significantly reduced with the subsequent arrests and trial that followed this attempt. While the defendants claimed they had intended only to kidnap de Gaulle, fifteen men faced a military trial (some *in absentia*) for their involvement, and all but one were imprisoned as a result. Bastien-Thiry was not so lucky, and faced a firing squad at the age of thirty-five for organising the plot, the last person in France to receive this form of execution.

Ten ways to (not) kill Castro

Fabian Escalante worked as the head of a counter-intelligence agency investigating CIA assassination plots against former Cuban president Fidel Castro. Escalante, whose job it was to protect Castro against these schemes, estimated that during the communist leader's years in political office, most notably between 1959 and 1965, he was the target of 638 plots to end his life. The popular revolution led by Fidel Castro in 1959, to take power away from CIA-favoured right-wing dictator Fulgencio Batista, saw the capitalist US influence on the island eradicated, and replaced with a communist regime that nationalised business and had good relations with the Soviet Union. An investigation into the assassination plots carried out by the CIA's Inspector General under President Lyndon B. Johnson's orders in 1967, produced a report (not approved for public release until 1993) that laid bare many of the ludicrous, extravagant and outlandish efforts the CIA considered going in their plans to assassinate Castro. Officially, these plots ceased in 1965 under President Johnson, but this didn't stop an attempt as recently as 2000 to kill Castro: one of the men arrested was a former CIA operative. Below are just some of the ways we now know Fidel Castro may have faced death.

— Perhaps the most famous assassination 'gadget' associated with Fidel Castro was the exploding cigar that was designed to blow up in the leader's face when he smoked it.

— A syringe filled with poison disguised as a Paper Mate pen was considered, with a needle so fine it was supposed to feel like nothing more than a scratch to the victim.

— Castro's passion for diving was also considered as a way to finish him off. One plan involved the Cuban being given, as a gift, a diving suit that had been contaminated with deadly bacteria, which would have caused a life-threatening skin infection.

— The CIA carried out a lot of research into Caribbean molluscs. A plan was suggested to fill a large seashell with explosives, and to paint it bright colours to attract Castro when he was diving.

— A handkerchief treated with liquid bacteria was considered. In fact, a number of things were considered as possible objects to be treated in this way, including Castro's tea and coffee, which he was known to drink regularly.

— Poisonous pills were also considered, but the CIA had some problems trying to create a lethal pill that dissolved effectively in water. The pills were tested on guinea pigs, who were unaffected by the toxin (later, it was discovered they had a natural immunity to it), and then on monkeys which died from it.

— The CIA offered $150,000 to a Mafioso to hire someone to carry out a hit on Castro, allegedly so the government could keep its hands clean. They supplied poisonous pills and arms to the men involved to help them carry out their plan. One plan failed when Castro stopped visiting a restaurant where they were planning to poison his food.

— Castro's former lovers were recruited to help kill him. One was given poisonous pills which she put in a jar of cream to conceal them. The pills dissolved so she was unable to go through with the plan. According to the woman, Castro had sensed that she was planning to kill him, and gave her a gun to finish him off, but she couldn't shoot him.

— In 2000, on a visit to Panama, Castro's security team uncovered 90kg of powerful explosives from under the podium where he was scheduled to speak. Four men were arrested and imprisoned as a result of the plot being foiled.

— Some earlier schemes, which seemed more likely to discredit or embarrass Castro than kill him, included spiking his cigars with drugs to make him behave absurdly in public, and filling the radio station where he broadcast his speeches with a substance that would have similar effects to LSD. The CIA report indicates that a plan to put a depilatory substance in Castro's shoes when he was on a trip out of the country, to make his beard fall out, was also considered.

Failed assassin
Name: Arthur Herman Bremer.
Profile: A native of Milwaukee, Wisconsin, Bremer was only twenty-one-years-old and working as a busboy at an upmarket

athletics club and an elementary school janitor's assistant, when he took action to assassinate a leading politician. Bremer grew up a fairly lonely child, and experienced some rejection from his first girlfriend, a fifteen-year-old who called him 'childish' and refused to attend pornographic movies with him. They broke up and, by January 1972, he had developed suicidal thoughts and began to entertain the idea of murder. Months before the attack, Bremer's behaviour had become more unusual — he shaved his head and was charged with possession of a concealed handgun. Although it was confiscated and he was fined, he was easily able to buy another weapon on 13 January 1972. This was the same day George Wallace declared his candidacy for the Democratic presidential nomination. By this point, Bremer had made a decision: rather than a random killing spree, he would track and assassinate a famous politician.

Target: George Wallace, Governor of Alabama. At the time of the attempt, Wallace was campaigning for the nomination to be the Democratic Party's presidential candidate.

Motive: It has never been made clear as to why Bremer decided to try and assassinate a political figure. He certainly was not fussy as to which politician it would be. In fact, President Nixon, who was campaigning for a second term, and Wallace's Democratic rival, George McGovern, were both considered by Bremer as possible victims, leading many to argue that there was no political motive behind the attempt. In the April prior to the attack on Wallace, Bremer travelled to Canada on Nixon's campaign trail, but was unable to carry out an attack, probably due to the large crowds and impressive security detail that followed the president wherever he went. It's likely that Wallace was selected because he was more of an easy target.

Time of attack: 3.58 p.m. on 15 May 1972.

Location: An open-air rally in Laurel, Maryland.

Plan of action: While Bremer may not have had a clear-cut reason for killing Wallace, he certainly made up for his lack of motive with his reconnaissance work. After the attack, police discovered he had spent five times his annual income on tracking and following Wallace around the country in the months leading up to 15 May. He was questioned by police two days before he tried to kill Wallace, for sitting in his car for ten hours outside an armoury where Wallace was due to speak. He told the cops he was there early to get a good seat, and they thought nothing more of it. On the day of the attack, Bremer first headed to Wheaton, Maryland, for a noon rally at a shopping mall, and then he travelled the 16 miles to Laurel for the afternoon appearance. He even went to the trouble of wearing a 'Wallace In '72' badge in the lapel of his jacket to blend in with the supporters. At the rally, he worked his way to the front of the crowds as Wallace finished addressing the audience from the podium.

What happened next: George Wallace had some controversial political views, especially regarding racial segregation, and on the morning of 15 May, he received an angry response from another Maryland audience. He had taken to wearing a bulletproof vest during public appearances but chose not to wear it in the afternoon because of how hot it was. Perhaps, surprisingly, he received a much more positive response in Laurel and, after he finished speaking, he removed his jacket and stepped down from the raised stage to meet the crowd. Bremer shouted out to Wallace, 'Hey, George, over here', and repeated the call until Wallace made his way close enough, and then Bremer pulled out his .38 revolver and fired at point-blank range, hitting the governor several times. As

Bremer was pounced upon by security, he continued to fire his weapon and hit three other people: a Secret Service agent, a journalist and one of Wallace's bodyguards.

Aftermath: Wallace was critically injured and spent five hours in surgery where doctors removed two bullets, one from his spine and one from his abdomen. Unfortunately, there was nothing they could do to repair the damage caused by the gunshot, and Wallace would be paralysed from the waist down for the rest of his life. He stepped down as a candidate for the Democratic presidential nomination but was later re-elected as Governor of Alabama. Arthur Bremer pleaded insanity during his trial, but this was rejected and he received a custodial sentence of sixty-three years (this was later reduced). He was released on 9 November 2007 at the age of fifty-seven, after serving thirty-five years.

Life imitating art, imitating life

Many people know that President Ronald Reagan's would-be assassin, John W. Hinckley Jr., was inspired to assassinate a leading political figure to impress Jodie Foster, one of the stars in Martin Scorsese's movie *Taxi Driver*, after watching the film a number of times. In the film, the central character Travis Bickle, played by Robert De Niro, plans to assassinate a fictional presidential candidate after becoming obsessed with one of the women on his campaign team. But what fewer people know is that, although Bickle never goes through with the shooting, as he is spotted by Secret Service, the man who inspired part of the character did. Screenwriter Paul Schrader said he drew on the real-life attempted assassination of George Wallace by Arthur Bremer when writing the film. It has been reported that Bremer himself was inspired to kill a politician after reading a book about Sirhan Sirhan, Robert F. Kennedy's assassin.

Park Chung-Hee (1917-79)

Longstanding South Korean President Park Chung-Hee was killed on 26 October 1979 by the chief of his own intelligence service, in a shocking attempt to overthrow him after he'd spent eighteen years in power. When the truth about Park's death was revealed, it came as a surprise to many that the people who ended his political career were not North Korean agents hoping to destabilise the South Korean government, but powerful South Koreans who disagreed with Park's leadership.

Perhaps the event was all the more surprising, given that the president had already survived two assassination attempts. The first took place in January 1968 when thirty-one North Korean commandos, dressed as South Korean soldiers, crossed the demilitarised zone and made it to within 800 metres of the Blue House, the presidential palace, before being questioned by police and blowing their cover by responding nervously to questions. The commandos fled, but most were tracked down and killed.

The more famous and closer call of the two attempts came six years later in 1974, when Park was giving a televised speech from the national theatre in celebration of the anniversary of his country's independence from Japan. Mun Se Gwang, who was believed to be a North Korean agent, fired at the president from the front row of the audience. He missed Park but killed Park's wife, Yuk Young Soo, and a student. Clearly surprised by the attack, Park acted unperturbed and continued with his speech while his wife was carried from the stage. The assailant was immediately tackled by the audience, and was executed for his crimes four months later.

An 'accidental' death

It was on 26 October 1979 that Park's number was finally up. His government originally claimed the event was an 'accidental' shooting, but it later emerged as a carefully engineered *coup* to end the president's regime. The assassination took place at a dinner party held in the president's honour at the Korean CIA's headquarters. The host was Kim Jae Kyu, the head of North Korea's intelligence service, who feared he might lose his job as the president was losing confidence in his judgement and no longer trusted his advice. The other guests were Cha Chi Chul, the chief of security and one of Park's closest advisers, whom Kim was known to disagree with, and staff secretary General Kim Kae Won. At the dinner, an argument erupted between Kim and Cha, and Kim left the room to retrieve a revolver. Later in the evening, he fired at Cha and President Park, who was hit three times, killing them both. When the president's bodyguards rushed to his defence, Kim's co-conspirators, who were also members of the Korean CIA, gunned them down. Kim gave himself up to the authorities and, along with four of the KCIA agents, was sentenced to death.

Pope John Paul II (1920-2005)

Every week, Pope John Paul II would make his way through St Peter's Square in Rome to bless the people who were gathered there to see him. The white open-topped car he was chauffeured in would drive slowly, stopping at regular intervals so the Pope, standing in the back of the vehicle, could reach out and touch the hands of the excited crowd. On 13 May 1981, he was going about this business as usual, when a man who appeared to be another excited well-wisher, reached up his arm, not to wave to the papal procession, but to fire four shots from a Browning 9mm gun at the Pope himself. Two of those shots hit two bystanders and the other two reached their target. The Pope collapsed, and the startled crowd apprehended the man, who was quickly identified as a twenty-three-year-old Turk named Mehmet Ali Agca, a wanted murderer who had escaped from a prison in his home country, where he was serving a sentence for killing the editor of a left-wing newspaper in 1979. It also transpired that he was a member of a fascist right-wing group called the Grey Wolves.

In the immediate aftermath of the assassination attempt, the Pope was rushed to hospital where doctors performed emergency surgery and, after some rest, he was back to good health, carrying out his many responsibilities. As for Ali Agca, he was convicted of attempted murder and given a life sentence. Initially, he claimed he had not been working for or with any other people in his planned attack, but after his conviction in 1982, he changed his story and claimed that the Bulgarian secret police, working in cahoots with the KGB, had paid him $1.25 million to kill the Pope. Prosecutors believed there was enough evidence in these wild claims to bring about a trial against four Turks and three Bulgarian alleged conspirators, with Ali Agca as the prosecution's key witness. When he took the stand, however, his inability to corroborate his story, lack of accurate details and the fact he blurted out remarkable statements such as, 'I am Jesus Christ!', made him an unreliable witness and the trial fell through. Agca served some of his sentence in Italy before being extradited to Turkey in 2000. He served the remainder of his sentence for the 1979 killing and was released in January 2010.

Failed assassin

Name: Marcus Sarjeant.

Profile: Aged only seventeen when he planned to kill the Queen, Sarjeant is one of the youngest wannabe assassins in this book. The former air cadet was from Capel-le-Ferne near Folkestone in Kent, and was later described as a shy loner. He considered himself somewhat of a failure and was obsessed with the high-profile deaths of John F. Kennedy and John Lennon, as well as the 1981 attempts on the lives of Ronald Reagan and Pope John Paul II, in March and May respectively of that year.

Target: Queen Elizabeth II.

Motive: Sarjeant wrote in his diary that he was going to stun the world with little more than a gun and planned to be the most famous teenager in the world for shooting the Queen. It was reported that he had joined an anti-royalist group, but his main motivation for the attack seemed to be the notoriety he would receive.

Time of attack: Just before 11 a.m., on 13 June 1981.

Location: Horse Guards Parade, near Buckingham Palace in London.

Plan of action: Sarjeant had tried to get a licence to buy a weapon that would fire live rounds and be capable of killing the Queen. He was unable to do so and settled for a blank-firing pistol instead, intending to simply scare Her Majesty.

What happened next: On that day in June, the Queen rode out of Buckingham Palace on her nineteen-year-old horse Burmese and headed down The Mall for the Trooping the Colour ceremony that traditionally takes place at Horse Guards Parade. The Mall was lined with tourists and onlookers hoping to catch a glimpse of the Queen as she rode by. She had taken fifteen minutes to make the journey and was just turning the corner into the Parade when Sarjeant fired six blank shots from the side of the road. The horse was startled, but the Queen quickly managed to control her steed and continued on the route as planned for the parade. Policemen and the Queen's Guards quickly apprehended Sarjeant, whose actions were caught on camera for all to see.

Aftermath: Sarjeant became the first person to be charged under the Treason Act 1842, for wilfully discharging at the person of Her Majesty the Queen, a blank cartridge pistol with intent to alarm her. He was found guilty and sentenced to five years in prison. While there, he wrote a letter to the Queen apologising for his behaviour, but never received a reply. After just over three years of his term, he was released and changed his name.

Bibliography

Books

Balsiger, David and Sellier Jr., Charles, *The Lincoln Conspiracy* (Schick Sunn Classic Books, 1977)

Belfield, Richard, *Terminate with Extreme Prejudice* (Robinson, 2005)

Cassels, Lavender, *The Archduke and the Assassin* (Stein and Day, 1984)

Clarke, James W., *American Assassins: The Darker Side of Politics* (Princeton University Press, 1982)

Di Eugenio, James and Pease, Lisa, *The Assassinations: Probe Magazine on JFK, MLK, RFK and Malcolm X* (Feral House, 2002)

Elliott, Paul, *Assassin!: The Bloody History of Political Murder* (Blandford, 1999)

Grant, R.G., *Assassinations: History's Most Shocking Moments of Murder, Betrayal and Madness* (Toucan Books, 2004)

Hudson, Miles, *Assassination* (Sutton Publishing Limited, 2000)

Krakauer, Jon, *Under the Banner of Heaven: A Story of Violent Faith* (Anchor Books, 2004)

Lentz, Harry M., *Assassinations and Executions: An Encyclopaedia of Political Violence, 1900 Through 2000* (McFarland and Co., 2002)

Mackay, Charles, *Mormons or Latter-day Saints: A Contemporary History* (Derby and Miller, 1852)

Malkin, Arthur Thomas, *The Gallery of Portraits with Memoirs: Volume III* (Charles Knight, 1833)

Menninger, Bonar, *Mortal Error: The Shot that Killed JFK* (Sidgwick and Jackson, 1992)

Miller, Scott, *The President and the Assassin: McKinley, Terror, and Empire at the Dawn of the American Century* (Random House, 2011)

Porter, Lindsay, *Assassination: A History of Political Murder* (The Overlook Press, 2010)

Sifakis, Carl, *Encyclopaedia of Assassinations* (Headline, 1993)

Treherne, Philip, *The Right Honourable Spencer Perceval* (T.F. Unwin, 1909)

Newspapers and Periodicals

Daily Mail
The Daily Telegraph
The Guardian
The Independent
LA Weekly
New Statesman
The New York Times
The Telegraph (Nashua)
Time

Websites

www.bbc.co.uk/news/
beck.library.emory.edu
www.catholic.org
www.cbsnews.com
civilwarwiki.net
www.eastview.com
www.fordham.edu
www.freerepublic.com
www.historyhouse.co.uk
www.historytoday.com
www.hueylong.com
www.jfklancer.com
law.umkc.edu
libcom.org
www.margaretthatcher.org
www.msnbc.msn.com
www.napoleonguide.com
www.newadvent.org
news.google.com
online.wsj.com
rt.com
www.theroyalforums.com

A NOTE TO THE READER

Dear Reader,

If you have enjoyed FAMOUS ASSASSINATIONS enough to leave a review on **Amazon** and **Goodreads**, then I would be truly grateful.

Sarah Herman

www.sarahherman.co.uk

Sapere Books is an exciting new publisher of brilliant fiction and popular history.

To find out more about our latest releases and our monthly bargain books visit our website:
saperebooks.com

Printed in Great Britain
by Amazon

44161173R00125